新媒体联盟地平线报告

（2013年博物馆版）

中英文版

美 国 新 媒 体 联 盟 **著**

中国科学技术协会科学技术普及部 **编译**

中国科学技术出版社

·北 京·

图书在版编目（CIP）数据

新媒体联盟地平线报告（2013年博物馆版）：中文、英文/美国新媒体联盟著；中国科学技术协会科学技术普及部编译 . —北京：中国科学技术出版社，2015.7

书名原文：*The NMC Horizon Report: 2013 Museum Edition*

ISBN 978-7-5046-6955-1

Ⅰ. ①新… Ⅱ. ①美… ②中… Ⅲ. ①博物馆学—文集—汉、英 Ⅳ. ① G260-53

中国版本图书馆 CIP 数据核字 (2015) 第 141303 号

The NMC Horizon Report＞2013 Museum Edition is a publication of The NMC（www.nmc.org）. Johnson, L., Adams Becker, S., Freeman, A., The NMC Horizon Report: 2013 Museum Edition. Austin, Texas: The New Media Consortium.

著作权合同登记号：01-2015-0232

本书简体中文版由美国新媒体联盟授权中国科学技术出版社独家出版，未经出版者许可不得以任何方式抄袭、复制或节录任何部分

策划编辑	许　慧　单　亭
责任编辑	单　亭　崔家岭
装帧设计	中文天地
责任校对	王勤杰
责任印制	张建农

出　　版	中国科学技术出版社
发　　行	科学普及出版社发行部
地　　址	北京市海淀区中关村南大街 16 号
邮　　编	100081
发行电话	010-62103130
传　　真	010-62179148
网　　址	http://www.cspbooks.com.cn

开　　本	787mm×1092mm　1/16
字　　数	150 千字
印　　数	1-5000 册
印　　张	6.5
版　　次	2015 年 7 月第 1 版
印　　次	2015 年 7 月第 1 次印刷
印　　刷	鸿博昊天科技有限公司
书　　号	ISBN 978-7-5046-6955-1 / G·684
定　　价	35.00 元

《新媒体联盟地平线报告》编译委员会

顾　　问	徐延豪　束　为　杨文志
主　　任	辛　兵
副 主 任	霍瑞娟　王欣华　胡富梅
委　　员	刘　俊　宋　宁　牛桂芹　张　章
	胡京波　马　骏　卢小戎　吴小林
	李伟元　刘晓婕　张　默　闫智勇
译　　者	霍菲菲　王　茜　刘　怡　张　章
	李晨光　张海波　郭万里　马新蕾
	杨士丽　杨　明
审　　定	辛　兵　欧建成

序　言

新媒体联盟（New Media Consortium）是一个非营利协会，主要关注新媒体和新技术的探索和使用。它的会员中很多是世界上著名的学院、大学和博物馆。近20多年来，该协会和它的会员们一直致力于为学习、研究和创新来探索和开发新兴技术。

《新媒体联盟地平线报告》是新媒体联盟地平线项目研究成果的一部分。地平线项目研究启动于2002年，旨在勾勒出影响全球教育领域的教、学以及创造性探究的新兴技术。每一年都会发布几类不同版本的地平线报告，分别聚焦于高等教育、基础教育和博物馆领域。截至2013年，新媒体联盟已发布了近30个版本的地平线报告，被翻译成多种文字在全球传播。

2010年，新媒体联盟与美国博物馆协会合作，开始发布《新媒体联盟地平线报告（博物馆版）》。检视未来五年有可能给全球范围博物馆教育及传播产生广泛影响的新兴技术，并对由此引发的博物馆教育发展的趋势及关键挑战进行了介绍。这标志着新技术与博物馆的融合研究正式进入更多研究者的视野，该项目研究过程经过严谨设计，成为教育技术研究关注的热点问题。在不严格区分博物馆、科技馆等内涵差异的情况下，各类场馆在教育技术应用方面具有相似性。新媒体技术给各类场馆的发展带来了重大的机遇和挑战。作为人类历史和文化的载体，包括科技馆在内的各类场馆必须顺应时代潮流，把技术和服务相结合，带动场馆向现代化发展。《新媒体联盟地平线报告（博物馆版）》对科技馆甚至整个科普领域都有重要的指导作用。

我国各类自然、历史、艺术和科技教育等场馆很多，但由于起步晚、底子薄，对新兴技术的接纳相对滞后，教育技术研发与应用存在盲目性，缺少针对性和前瞻性。针对这种情况，我们准备以编译《新媒体联盟地平线报告

（2013年博物馆版）》（*The NMC Horizon Report: 2013 Museum Edition*）为起点，引入先进的科普理念，提升科普工作人员的自身技能，真正培养出一批高水平、具有创新能力的科普专业人才。同时，随着新技术的不断应用，还需要拥有一批素质过硬的新媒体技术专家，从而建立起专兼结合，以专职为核心，兼职为主体的团队，唯有如此，才能够真正把深奥的科学知识通过妙趣横生的技术手段表现出来，并能够根据形势不断创新，推动我国科技馆事业迈向一个新的台阶。

《新媒体联盟地平线报告（2013年博物馆版）》编译委员会
2015年2月

目 录

序　言	
概　要	1
主要趋势	6
重大挑战	8
BYOD	11
众　包	17
电子出版	23
位基服务	29
自然用户界面	34
保护与修护技术	40
新媒体联盟地平线项目简介	46
研究方法	48
新媒体联盟地平线项目：2013年博物馆版咨询委员会名单	51

英文版

Executive Summary	55
Key Trends	59
Significant Challenges	61
Time-to-Adoption Horizon: One Year or Less	
> BYOD	63
> Crowdsourcing	69
Time-to-Adoption Horizon: Two to Three Years	
> Electronic Publishing	73
> Location-Based Services	77
Time-to-Adoption Horizon: Four to Five Years	
> Natural User Interfaces	81
> Preservation and Conservation Technologies	85
The NMC Horizon Project	91
Methodology	93

概　要

国际公认的全球研究报告《新媒体联盟地平线报告》和以地区为焦点的《新媒体联盟技术展望》系列出版物是"新媒体联盟地平线项目"的组成部分。前者着眼于全球性研究，后者则以区域性研究为主。该研究项目始于2002年，旨在预测和描述继每一版系列出版物出版后的5年内可能会对全球正式和非正式教育产生重大影响的新兴技术。《新媒体联盟地平线报告（2013年博物馆版）》探究了博物馆环境内新兴技术在教育和传播方面的潜在影响及应用。我们希望该报告对全球博物馆产生借鉴意义，国际化结构的咨询委员会反映了一种全球视角。影响新兴技术在博物馆的采纳和使用不仅有众多地区因素，而且还有一些跨国界因素。鉴于这些挑战，我们提出了这篇报告。《新媒体联盟地平线报告（2013年博物馆版）》是新媒体联盟（NMC）与马库斯数字艺术教育学院(MIDEA)联合出版的年度博物馆系列报告的第四份报告。

《新媒体联盟地平线报告》共有三个全球版本——高等教育版、基础教育版（幼儿园到12年级）和博物馆教育版。每个版本都着重介绍了在未来五年内在其目标领域可能成为主流的六类新兴技术或做法，及会对同一时期内现行做法产生影响的主要趋势和挑战构成了这些讨论的框架。

《新媒体联盟地平线报告（2013年博物馆版）》列出了6项技术，分为三个预期采纳与应用阶段，揭示出它们成为博物馆教育和传播主流应用的时间框架。近期阶段假定在未来一年内成为博物馆主流应用的可能性；中期阶段指2~3年期间，远期阶段则是指4~5年期间。需要注意的是,《新媒体联盟地平线报告》并不是预测工具，而是强调在博物馆教育和传播上具有巨大应用潜力的新兴技术。报告中所列的6项技术中的每一个技术都已经成为世界上很多创新型博物馆和组织的工作目标，我们在此展示的项目和展项揭示了更广泛的潜在影响。

短期阶段

未来12个月内"自带移动设备"和"众包"将迅速成为博物馆教育的两大技术主题，包括参观者深层介入博物馆的方法。借助这两种技术，参观者可以将博物馆藏品的相关信息储存到自带的移动设备里，也可以分享自己对展品的观点和感想，而这些参观者个人的想法也可能成为展品信息的一部分。"自带设备"很大程度上源于博物馆员工的办公需求，因为越来越多的员工希望能用装有自己喜欢的高效办公软件的个人笔记本电脑工作。"众包"并不是一个新概念，但当众包同社交媒体和众筹网站结合起来时，大众就可在展览开发、展品目录设计以及展品资料库完善方面发挥更加积极的作用。

> **自带移动设备**是为最大限度地提高工作效率。越来越多的人随身携带笔记本电脑或者其他移动办公设备，"自带移动设备"也应运而生。通过"自带设备"的方式，各种组织机构纷纷摒弃以往自上而下提供技术手段以提高工作效率的做法，开始为员工个人计算机设备的使用提供网络服务和环境框架支持。随着越来越多的人在生活中使用智能手机导航，博物馆借助个人移动设备吸引参观者的前景十分广阔。很多博物馆提供移动应用程序为参观者提供导览、信息共享和展览规划服务，大大减轻了博物馆大批采购此类服务设备租借给参观者的压力。由于工作人员都在用个人电脑进行日常工作，博物馆内部的工作流程也因自带移动设备而改变。在多数软件均从网上下载、网络技术无处不在的时代，自带移动设备的发展前景将越来越好，

因此，对于博物馆来说，最好的选择就是成为自带移动设备应用的先锋，并享有制定规则的权利等先驱优势。

> **众包**是指利用群体的想法和劳动从而实现共同目标的一套方法。维基百科是众包最著名的案例，成千上万的志愿者依托一个开放的网络平台，共同分担编排历史研究和当代研究的重任。很多博物馆利用众包方式，通过社交媒体来提高社区在博物馆活动中的参与度，鼓励参观者提供自己的感想和相关视频，增加博物馆活动与展览中的互动。众包前景最看好的方面之一是它藉由众多个体提供小额资金来资助小型或大型项目的能力。2012年，通过众筹网站 Kickstarter 为艺术相关项目筹集到的资金首次超过了美国国家艺术基金会的筹资额。除了募集资金以外，文化机构也通过此方式为亟待介绍的艺术品和文物藏品征集元数据，其中包括为视障人士提供 alt 替代文本。

中期阶段

第二个预期应用范围是在未来2~3年，电子出版和定位服务两大科技将有望超过《地平线项目》规定的20%应用率，成为地平线项目框架的主流技术。随着共享展品目录、博物馆专用应用程序以及其他富媒体出版物、互动型出版物的呼声越来越高，电子出版正在改变全世界博物馆的工作流

程。定位服务可根据参观者的个人喜好，为其提供导览。定位技术快速发展已成定势，包括苹果和谷歌在内的大公司都开始纷纷收购专业从事智能定位和室内导航技术研发的新成立的小公司。

> **电子出版** 在媒体、科研、新闻以及小说等方面的消费方式上正在掀起翻天覆地的变化。像《纽约时报》(*The New York Times*) 和《新闻周刊》(*Newsweek*) 这些主要传媒公司，正在为电子出版的未来发展确立标准。丰富多彩的媒体资源，如视频、图像、音频等，这些数字构件模块可以很容易地应用于各种媒体格式，服务于不同的受众对象，这一思想对于拓宽博物馆内容的覆盖面具有巨大意义。总体而言，文化机构在向电子出版工作流程的转型过程中还有许多工作要做，包括采用设计流程，将数字媒体用于多种传播渠道。"盖蒂博物馆在线学术展品目录计划"(The Getty's Online Scholarly Catalogue Initiative) 为博物馆媒体制作的现代化提供了所需的工具和框架，使在线出版成为博物馆的首要工作。下一步是要研发可持续的系统，用于管理和重新定位数字资源，同时进行内容设计，以适应不同的移动平台。

> **位基服务** 已经融入大众生活，人们运用移动手机应用程序去寻找自己所处的方位，这已经成为一种不假思索的下意识行为。由于有无线局域网络(WiFi)、全球定位系统(GPS)，增强型无线电频率识别(RFID) 标码以及诸如社交地图(Waze) 这样的众包定位技术的支持，现在定位服务不仅可以精准定位(甚至室内定位)，还能够提供该位置相关的最新信息。拥有几年发展史的社交定位软件"四方定位"(FourSquare)，已经成为这一技术可以如何无缝地应用于个人生活的最成功的范例之一，用户每公布和分享一次自己的地理位置都会获得相应的积分奖励。对于博物馆来说，定位服务应用软件与其他技术，可以通过伴随的数字互动显示屏与专门设置成为参观者的向导，帮助他们找到自己喜爱的展品或为他们建议最佳参观路线。博物馆专家和应用程序研发人员发现，在博物馆提供定位服务能够为参观者带来一段难忘的、意义非凡的文化体验。

远期阶段

就远期来看，即4~5年进入主流应用的应该是"自然用户界面"和"保护与修护技术"。"自然用户界面"可对用户的触摸、移动、声音以及面部表情做出反应，采用此项技术的展览可以给参观者带来更直观的体验，为用户提供与艺术作品和艺术装置互动的机会。多年以来，博物馆专业人员一直在探索如何能够保护和修复因技术日新月异的进步而有过时之虞的实物和数字藏品。除了记录艺术家的创作初衷外，确立开发和归档元数据的工作流程也将是保护和修复藏品工作的关键。这两项技术离进入主流应用尚需几年时间，但已经显而易见，这些技术对博物馆的影响将意义深远。这两项技术引起了人们极大的兴趣，吸引了大量投资，足已证明它们值得密切关注。

> **自然用户界面**　由于融触摸、声音和手势动作识别于一体的新平台的出现，自然用户界面拉近了人与电脑的距离。智能手机和平板电脑用户对自然用户界面带来的轻松操作体验再熟悉不过了。然而，触摸屏之外的技术在飞速发展，使得人机交互更加直观。人们不再使用触摸屏，而是通过安装在智能手机上的虚拟助手来请求查询和接收信息、发送文本和邮件，或者使用定位数据，这已经不是什么新鲜事情了。这些新技术迫使博物馆重新思考参观者与艺术品和文物展品之间的互动方式，而如今有相当一部分博物馆已经安装了平板电脑和多点触屏，帮助观众重新创造展品，使它们融入展览。微软公司研制的 Kinect 设备，是一项应用运动传感器的基于手势的技术。该设备被博物馆越来越多地采用，以鼓励参观者与各种精美展品的数字演示进行互动，此技术已经越来越多地在博物馆里得到应用。自然用户界面技术最新的成果，是将纹理融入原来的普通触摸屏，从而使用户感受到各种触觉刺激。总而言之，自然用户界面为博物馆创造了利用新兴技术的机会，使参观者能够更加深度地参与到艺术品和文物藏品中。

《新媒体联盟地平线报告》共有三个全球版本——高等教育版、基础教育版（幼儿园到 12 年级）和博物馆教育版，每个版本都着重介绍了未来五年在其目标领域可能成为主流的六类新兴技术和做法。

> **保护与修护技术**　虽然"保护"与"修护"这两个词常常被混用，但就两者的目的而言，是完全不同的两个概念。保护者们是通过保护文物的意图与介质来防止其过时；而修护者们则是对日久容易遭受破坏的文物进行修护和还原。数字档案就是第一个由展品保护人员实施的技术解决方案，并自此产生了专业人才的一个新标准。根据这个新标准，他们既要精通档案学理论，又要具备开发元数据管理工具的专业知识。除了把易损文物数字化外，在以往利用过时技术制作的时基媒体数字展品的保护上，负责保护文化遗产的人们还面临着一系列的难题。对现代保护者而言，最主要的挑战就是如何以忠实于艺术家创作意图且可操作的方式呈现艺术内容。由于科技进步，数字和实体文物的保护和修护技术变得日趋成熟，诸如美国国会图书馆这样的一些机构正在制定维护文化遗产完整性创新方法的标准。

为了编写本年度报告，由博物馆、教育、科技以及其他领域的国际专家团队组成了一个咨询委员会。经过 2013 年 8 月至 9 月期间的讨论，2013 年新媒体联盟博物馆咨询委员会在《新媒体联盟地平线报告（2013 年博物馆版）》应涉及的主题上最终达成共识。每一个主题下的实例和阅读材料旨在提供实用的模式及更详细的信息。

本报告的正文部分对六大新兴技术做了详细叙述，包括该项技术是什么、为什么与博物馆教育和传播息息相关。我们的研究表明，六大新兴技术都能够明确地应用于博物馆教育和传播。本报告旨在以简单、引人入胜的方式对其进行叙述。

咨询委员会针对一系列研究问题展开讨论，以揭示博物馆教育和传播实践中的重要发展趋势和挑战，为该报告辨别可能应用于博物馆领域的新兴技术。本报告参考了丰富的资源，包括最新的研究成果以及地平线项目团队和咨询委员会成员的专业实践。咨询委员会成员之间开展的互动是《新媒体联盟地平线报告（2013 年博物馆版）》的研究重点，本报告详细介绍了专家一致认可的各技术领域。详细的研究方法在本报告的结尾处列出。

2014 年，咨询委员会由来自 6 个国家的 44 名技术专家组成，名单附在报告的后面。尽管专家们背景不同，实践经验各异，但他们一致认为，本报告中涉及的每一个技术主题都会在未来 5 年内对全球的博物馆教育和传播产生重大的影响。对这些技术应用的兴趣起到推动作用的主要趋势以及博物馆为了最大限度地发挥潜能必须应对的挑战，这些也代表了咨询委员会专家们的视角；同时也是《新媒体联盟地平线报告（2013 年博物馆版）》接下来一节的关注点。

为了便于对比，每一年、每一版的《新媒体联盟地平线报告》都采用相同的格式，报告开篇都会探讨咨询委员会认定的未来 5 年最重要的趋势和挑战。本版报告主体部分的格式密切反映出"地平线项目"的一个关注重点——新兴技术在博物馆的应用。报告的每个部分都首先概述相关技术主题，然后讨论该技术与博物馆教育和传播的关系，同时辅以如何应用相关技术的具体实例。

最后，每一部分的结尾会提供带有注解的推荐阅读材料和补充案例，进一步拓展报告所讨论的内容。所有这些资源及广泛收集的其他有益项目和阅读材料都可以在该项目的开放内容数据库中查到。该数据库可以通过新媒体联盟地平线项目 EdTech 应用程序进入。iOS 用户通过 go.nmc.org/ios 登陆，安卓（Android）用户通过 go.nmc.org/android 登陆。《新媒体联盟地平线报告（2013 年博物馆版）》的所有背景材料（包括研究数据、主题初选、主题预览和最新刊登的研究报告）都可以在 iTunes U 上免费下载（go.nmc.org/itunes-u）。

主要趋势

每一年度《新媒体联盟地平线报告》中介绍的技术，无论是在博物馆领域还是在全球范围内，都与其所处的时代紧密相连。为确保能够更好地理解我们所处的时代特征，咨询委员会对大量现有文章、访谈、论文和最新研究进行了广泛调研，以确定目前影响博物馆教育和传播实践的趋势，并对这些趋势进行排序。趋势列表确定后，根据未来五年内每种趋势对博物馆可能的重要性进行排序。得到咨询委员会成员广泛认同的趋势会排在最前面，它们被认为是 2013 年到 2018 年间推动博物馆技术应用的关键因素。根据咨询委员会的评估，这些趋势的排列顺序为：

1. **跨机构协作将成为资源共享的重要途径**。博物馆越来越意识到如何在更广阔的网络环境中共享和使用信息，包括但不仅限于非媒体化藏品数据。那个规模庞大、费时多年、由基金会资助的合作项目的年代已经过去。数据层面的多机构合作越来越多地出现，其中许多机构只作为消极意义上的合作伙伴，而整合多方资源的真正工作则很可能由第三方组织在下游完成。

2. **与藏品相关的"富媒体"越来越成为数字传播的宝贵资产**。博物馆逐渐发现，通过制定适当策略，利用一切机会采集高品质媒体文件极具价值。研究人员和内容专家与教育和技术专家展开从未有过的紧密合作，抓住使用数字资源带来的机会，促进线上和场馆实地的多模式学习。视频、音频和动画不再是解说的补充，而逐渐成为传播计划中不可或缺的一部分。这种趋势对博物馆专业人员和参观者而言都是有益的，因为它能够加深对陈列品、内涵以及对观众的理解。

3. **数字化和编目项目不断需要博物馆资源的深度共享**。博物馆的特色在于其保存的内容和对内容的解读。博物馆专业人员逐渐认识到，参观者希望能够轻松地获取准确而有趣的信息和高品质媒体。这要求博物馆制定藏品数字化和编目的战略规划。为实现长远目标，这些项目经常要牺牲紧缺资源（如资金、人力或时间）。

4. **对市民和社会参与的期待深刻改变着博物馆的视界、范围和关系。**博物馆越来越多地采用社交媒体、开放内容和众包等新兴科技和方法来加深其所在社区从内到外的参与。应用这些创新意味着博物馆为观众提供了更多的浸入式机会去成为展品内容的一部分。逐渐地,不能亲临博物馆参观的人们也能够欣赏到博物馆藏品,并对关于在实体场馆中开展的活动的讨论作出有意义的回应和积极建言献策,从而重新定义了博物馆观众的意涵。

博物馆开始重视制定正式策略,利用一切机会采集高质量媒体文本。

5. **观众和工作人员越来越期待获得跨设备的无缝体验。**无论是参观场馆里的陈列品、订票,还是逛在线商店,或只是浏览博物馆网站,观众都期待博物馆能提供更多的数字资源和内容,并希望可以通过个人设备实现与这些内容的持续互动。虚拟参观者尤其希望能够快速、简单地在线完成一些典型任务,而不论手头上使用的是什么设备。对于实地参观者也是如此,经常会看到人们通过查看智能手机来决定接下来参观展馆的哪一部分。

6. **人们越来越希望随时随地利用社交网络进行工作、学习、研究和联系。**当我们希望用电脑时,不必局限于电脑桌前。雇员们越来越希望能在家中或上班的途中工作,并且,几乎所有人都希望能够随时随地获得信息、查阅地址、路线、文献和答案。对于博物馆专业人士和博物馆观众来说,这都是一个主要的趋势。从远足到出差,通过移动设备获取信息的可能性正在改变我们制订计划的方式。这种趋势使人们随时随地都能很方便地上网。

7. **所有博物馆相关领域对数据基本能力的需求都在增加。**世界上 90% 的数据都是过去两年间产生的,由于硬件、软件和网络的指数式增长,每天还会增加 2.5×10^{18} 字节。在不久的将来,重大社会决定需要大数据的支撑,而对于富有知识的公民个人来说,如果想要充分参与到这些对话讨论中来,就必须具备阅读和解读大数据的能力。另外在美国,五分之一的人不使用互联网,原因包括缺乏知识、负担不起电脑和互联网的费用或不了解其内在价值。这些人将会面临落后于数据发展的危机,而图书馆和博物馆则有机会延伸服务至这些群体,确保其获得 21 世纪成功人士所必需的数据基本技能。

重大挑战

任何关于技术应用的讨论都必须考虑重要的约束和挑战，咨询委员会对当前事件、论文、文章和类似资源进行了详尽分析，并根据个人经验详细说明了博物馆在采用新技术过程中面临的一连串挑战。下面详细说明了一些重要挑战，但是很显然在这些挑战背后存在着一种普遍的共识：博物馆自身当中固有的约束条件很可能是决定其是否采用某一项特定技术的最重要因素。

即使是渴望采用新技术的机构也可能受到人力匮乏和资金短缺的严重限制而无法实现这些想法。还有一些博物馆位于建筑物中，而这些建筑物设计之初并没有考虑到无线技术需要的射频透过性，因此它们与许多潜在的技术选项无缘。虽然认识到许多自身因素会严重影响技术的应用，但是咨询委员会将其研究聚焦在对博物馆以及整个博物馆界共同的挑战上。

以下为咨询委员会总结的博物馆采用新兴技术面临的挑战，由高到低排序如下：

1. **需要深入理解博物馆内应用的技术与面向大众的技术（例如网站、社交媒体和移动应用）之间的关系、差异和协同效应。** 很少有博物馆管理人员能够看到博物馆虚拟参观者可能带来的募款、慈善和专业化营销机会。现实和虚拟的博物馆参观者之间的界限正日益模糊，而他们都非常希望在线获取服务和信息。必须提供综合的在线信息和服务是博物馆面临的一个现实挑战，尤其是对于小型博物馆而言更是如此。对于大型博物馆，提供这类服务已经是参观者认为理所应当的事情。

2. **各种规模的博物馆正在努力适应科技影响下重新定义职员职责和组织机构。** 技术在博物馆各方面的广泛应用极大影响了数字部门的重要性；现在他们需要同时进行水平式工作（与其他部门进行协调和互动）和垂直式工作（必要的领导和战略监督）。此外，由于从教育、营销到研究、策划，数字化触及博物馆的各个领域，这些活动开始不被严格区分，变得相互交融。

顺应这样的转变不仅需要数字小组掌握新技术，还需要整个机构的新技术。比如，泰特博物馆正在进行全面的机构改革，重点打造博物馆的数字化战略。

3．**全面的数字化战略是机构长期可持续发展计划至关重要的部分。** 这种战略不仅包括技术计划的传统元素（如硬件、软件，网络等），同时也应该包括数字化营销、慈善以及创收；还包括数字化、数字保护和长期的技术基础设施建设等关键任务。这项计划应包括所有基础设施需求，以尽可能使博物馆能为未来发展留足空间。另外，博物馆显然不能简单地像策划一份折页或展品目录册那样去策划其网络存在。当今博物馆的数字化不仅有网站，还有社交媒体、移动工具和应用程序、虚拟社区互动、电子集资，网络销售等。所有这些以及所涉及的技术问题都必须予以考虑、解决。

4．**多数情况下，博物馆可能不具备必需的技术设施来实现数字化学习的愿景。** 仅在美国，就有大约 17000 个机构自我认定为博物馆；然而其中很多机构的员工短缺，资源稀少。在现今这个互联网时代，人们已经意识到数字化学习的价值，但是多数博物馆的现状是不具备实现数字化学习所必需的技术基础设施，并且通常没有时间来明确自己的愿景，更别说实现这一愿景了。而那些资源相对丰富的博物馆则需要把非数字化教育资金进行重新分配，以完成所需的技术基础设施。

制定一个综合的、可持续的数字资产管理策略比以往任何时候都显得更加重要，只有这样才能满足高效创建、管理、发现和传递数据的需求。

5．**残疾人群在总人口和博物馆参观人群的比重增加，博物馆对于残疾人群的无障碍参观需要认真考虑。** 美国有超过 5000 万的残疾人，博物馆需要继续改善设施、展览内容和教育活动，使这部分群体能够更方便地参观和使用展馆设备。为了方便这类群体，博物馆正在更多地思考教育活动和教育材料呈现的方式。技术的应用有助于打破障碍。例如，触摸技术能让失明或视力局部残疾的人触摸虚拟的 3D 物品。另外，博物馆可以通过为那些自带先进技术设备的残疾观众提供特别内容去弥补这一鸿沟。

6．**在创造管理、部署藏品信息和数字资产的可持续发展环境方面，博物馆做得还不够。** 藏品信息的终端和平台的快速发展变得难以支撑和维持，包括文本、网络、音频、视频、图像文件的藏品数据和数字资产等被多地保存，且大多相互不连接，常导致信息冲突。因此，制定一个综合、可持续的数字资产管理策略变得比以往任何时候都显得更加重要，只有这样才能满足高效创建、管理、发现和传送数字材料的需求。

这些趋向和挑战反映了技术对我们生活的几乎各个层面和对整个博物馆界的影响；同时，表明我们的交流沟通、信息获取、联系同事和好友、学习甚至社交方式的本质都在发生变化。

在 NMC 地平线报告项目研究的背景下，这些趋势和挑战给咨询委员会提供了一个框架，通过该框架衡量近 50 个新兴技术及做法的潜在影响，经过分析和讨论决定哪些可以纳入本期的 NMC 地平线报告。其中的六个关键技术，在报告的主体部分予以详细介绍。

BYOD
预期投入应用时间：1 年以内

BYOD，即"自带设备"，是指人们携带自己的设备，包括笔记本电脑、平板电脑、智能手机等进入学习环境。BYOD 这个术语是英特尔公司于 2009 年首创的，因为他们发现公司的员工越来越多地使用自己的设备接入公司网络。自此之后，这种模式在全球的工作场所司空见惯。BYOD 在博物馆领域的发展源于许多机构缺少资金和基础设施，不足以给每一位员工和志愿者提供设备，更不要说给观众了。而 BYOD 则可以利用人们已有的设备。早期研究证明，使用个人设备的个体行为，其生产效率和参与度都得到了极大提升。平板电脑的功能日益强大（现已有更多品牌可供选择，如 iPad、Galaxy、Nexus 和 Surface），在 BYOD 领域具备得天独厚的条件。

概述

对于博物馆和其他教育机构来说，自带设备与其说是指设备，倒不如说是指用户已经加载到设备上的个性化内容。很少有两个设备共享完全相同的内容和设置，自带设备使得个人利用这些工具实现自己的效率和生产力最大化。如今，把用户与他们的设备和应用程序分离就像把他们与属于自己的最珍贵的财物分离一样。此种设备已经成为个人工作和学习环境的路径，有丰富的互动功能，能促进探索新学科，让不论身在何处的人彼此互联互通。从这个意义上讲，工作环境已经超越了员工被拴在办公桌旁或局限在一个物理空间的概念，通过互联网及其大量可下载的应用程序开启了无限生产效率潜能。

自带设备这一概念起源于英特尔 2010 年启动的一个个人设备项目。如今，这一项目支持着英特尔员工的 25000 部智能手机，据英特尔自己称，每天都为员工增加将近 1 小时的生产效率，同时还能提升士气。英特尔使以往的机构对技术的决策权和所有权模式变成由员工自由决定和选择。

对于博物馆的工作人员，自带设备政策促进了工作环境中拥有更多的自由和灵活性，并排除了不安全设备的隐患。越来越多的人员选择自己带笔记本电脑去博物馆，即使他们不在工作大楼，也可以使他们顺利地完成任务。

这种自带设备给博物馆工作人员带来的便捷性也促使我们考虑利用它来改进观众的参观体验。传统博物馆提供给顾客录音导览设备伴随参观，现在则鼓励人们在该空间内使用个人智能手机或平板电脑。这种转变很大程度上是由于移动应用程序的快速扩散——这也许是移动领域发展最快的一个方面。应用程序是设备个性化的关键推手，因为用户可以从与他们的工作和兴趣最密切相关的大量教育和生产资源中进行选择。

来自高德纳公司最近的一份报告预测，在 2013 年有 1020 亿次应用程序被下载，或者说地球上的每个人要下载近 15 次应用程序。截至 2013 年 10 月，定期更新的在线应用程序计数器 148Apps 显示，仅在 iTunes 商店，就有超过 86000 个活跃的教育应用程序，使教育成为排在游戏后的第二大最受欢迎的类别。很多博物馆，尤其是大型博物馆，正在利用这种驱动力，创建它们自己的应用程序，通过录音导览和辅助资料来增强自带设备观众的体验，同时也将学习活动和互动体验延伸至博物馆的物理空间之外。

与博物馆教育及传播的关联性

移动设备的激增，以及越来越多的移动应用程序，对博物馆的移动策略产生着巨大的影响，包括创建移动网站和应用程序、提供免费无线上网，或者为馆内设备上的导览扩充可用于观众自带设备上的内容。这一改变值得注意，因为它将会转变博物馆资源，包括从维护和提供技术到高质量的多媒体体验内容及其交付。这一改变虽然不是完全取代传统的由博物馆提供移动设备的做法，但却是一个包含有大量馆内活动的领域。

一方面，博物馆参观者期望无缝连接随时随地能上网；另一方面，要求博物馆提供免费无线上网——这是自带设备成为可行的关键——背后的主要推手却是博物馆员工。博物馆越来越多地聘用合同工和临时工，他们需要利用自己的设备进行工作。即便在博物馆提供设备的情况下，通常员工自己的设备也比博物馆提供的设备质量更优。很多员工渴望在展厅内工作，一个公开访问的无线信号是至关重要的。参观者还可以方便地连接网络访问他们的社交网络，在博物馆之外进行拓展研究，并使用由博物馆设计的移动应用程序去增强他们的博物馆现场体验。

更多的博物馆从参观者能在他们的设备上拥有和定制博物馆内容方面看到了价

值，因为它是为连接博物馆内部和外部教育和传播迈出的重要一步。普拉多博物馆的官方指南通过参观者在参观前、参观中和参观后个性化学习体验体现了当前移动应用程序的潮流。移动应用程序可以给学习者提供高品质艺术品的图像，并可定制专题参观，进行可搜索的索引，直接访问、进入普拉多博物馆的Facebook和Twitter账户。

无处不在的带有专业相机功能的智能手机和社交应用程序已经影响到博物馆如何在馆内空间接待使用这些设备的参观者。如今，场馆内设置屏幕以利用社交媒体源鼓励参观者之间对话这种做法已司空见惯。在澳大利亚的当代艺术博物馆有一个叫MCA NOW的正式活动，它通过参观者和员工把Instagram和Twitter交流信息显示在各楼层显示器上，来共享博物馆的故事。摄影的冲动也正在被几家大型博物馆机构所认可，其中包括纽约大都会艺术博物馆、印第安纳波利斯艺术博物馆和盖蒂博物馆，它们放宽了政策，允许对部分或所有的展览拍摄，这是对不断发展的自带设备趋势的直接回应。

尽管越来越多的博物馆已经修改关于接受观众自带设备的政策，但是尚不普遍。许多博物馆都与运营商签订了长期合同，因为安全、费用或基础设施问题，为观众提供免费的无线网络也存在局限性。一些博物馆仍然存储和供应设备，因为这样比通过跨越大量平台建设和支持一个强大的本地应用程序更便宜。创建高效的在任何设备上都能运行的数字解说文件是博物馆目前正在解决之中的一个挑战。许多博物馆正在尝试改造自己的网站，通过配备响应式设计或构建移动网站来避免平台可访问性问题。最终，随着博物馆越来越接受自带设备，提供免费无线网络将成为一个需要考虑的重要步骤。

博物馆中自带设备功能举例：

> **展览和藏品** 克利夫兰艺术博物馆的"艺术透镜"应用的是一个iPad应用程序，它允许参观者在馆内或家中进一步探索藏品。包含的应用程序有室内寻路技术，将观众带领到有视频和电影解说内容的艺术品那里，同时提供扫描功能，可以识别某一个图像并提供与之相关的内容：go.nmc.org/artl。

> **营销和公共关系** 营销部门在特别活动中应用自带设备，提供背景幕布和照相亭，鼓励游客通过社交媒体分享他们的博物馆体验。墨西哥艺术博物馆经常在展览空间创建特殊区域，让观众进行自拍，以再现部分艺术作品：go.nmc.org/mexic。

> **观众服务和无障碍服务** 博物馆使用专门为移动设备设计的应用程序可以方便聋哑人参观。SzépMűSL是一款最近由

布达佩斯的美术博物馆创建的安卓和 iOS 应用程序，它的特点是为博物馆收藏的约 150 幅油画配有几种国际手语解说视频：go.nmc.org/szep.

自带设备的应用实例

下面的链接是自带设备在博物馆及其他环境中投入应用的实例：

带上你的智能手机

go.nmc.org / DMAA

达拉斯艺术博物馆网站告诉观众带上智能手机，以便更好访问专门为该馆馆藏精选作品开发的内容。该馆还有覆盖全馆的免费无线网络，鼓励参观者把他们的笔记本电脑和其他移动设备带到"互联网咖啡馆"去。

自带设备应用于时装技术学院（PDF）

go.nmc.org / fitnewyork

位于纽约的时装技术学院（FIT）已经实施了强大、安全的无线网络，每年使一万名以上的学生、教师和工作人员以及超过 10 万名的博物馆参观者可以自带移动设备。其目的是消除对有线计算机实验室的需求，同时保持宽带的质量，以创建更加高效、灵活的工作空间。

自带设备可保持医疗集团的竞争优势

go.nmc.org / nchhealth

NCH 卫生系统，是一家在佛罗里达州的医院集团，为其两部分业务实施了一个由两部分组成的自带设备策略，努力促进高效、无纸化的工作环境。为了提供最大便利，管理者允许员工使用自己的设备，同时在招聘医生时利用这种自带设备政策来取得竞争优势。

自带设备为 VMware 公司节省 200 万美元

go.nmc.org / vmware

软件公司 VMware 公司是自带设备的先驱，自 2011 年第四季度采用了这种做法以来，该公司凭借为员工报销 IT 费用的有效制度，仅在移动电话方面节省了 200 万美元。该结余被分配用于改善基础设施和研发项目。

夺取博物馆

go.nmc.org/scot

苏格兰国家博物馆开发了一项活动，它要求参观者下载"夺取博物馆"应用程序到自己的手机来注册一个实地的团队游戏，该游戏要求玩家探索展厅以宣布自己所夺取的领地。该应用程序的开发是为了增强参观者的参与和促进新一代博物馆观众的参与度。

MCA 的洞察力

go.nmc.org / MCA

澳大利亚当代艺术博物馆开发了一个

"MCA 的洞察力"应用程序，为博物馆的收藏提供一个互动辅助解说功能，鼓励观众通过视频和图像去探索艺术作品和艺术装置背后的故事。该应用程序还包括一个位置感知系统，通过响应式地图帮助用户找到他们的路径。

测验之路

go.nmc.org / mid

伦敦泰特美术馆的"测验之路"应用程序可以引导参观者按照主题参观路线（包括从"动物"到"神话传说"等主题）来参观展馆，根据每次旅程所回答正确的问题数量，可以获得奖品和折扣。通过设计该应用程序，让儿童和成人参与沉浸式的挑战，并了解英国的艺术。

扩展阅读

如想了解更多有关自带设备方面的内容，建议参详以下文章和资源：

2013 年四大自带设备趋势

go.nmc.org / byodinfo

（迈克尔·恩德勒，《信息周刊》，2013年 2 月 21 日）根据高德纳公司关于自带设备在企业中的影响的评估，该作者强调四大趋势，涉及各行业每一个 IT 领导者，包括以自带设备作为招聘工具的安全性及其使用。

自带设备：对于成功实施的六点技巧

go.nmc.org / success

（山姆·甘嘎，《数据中心期刊》，2013年 10 月 7 日）相关组织在制定一个成功的自带设备政策时必须考虑许多因素，包括安全性与技术关切问题以及创建一个监管模式来解决新出现的问题。本文提供了一个问题及要点列表，指出的都是制定和实施自带设备政策需考虑的相关问题。

亲爱的博物馆：接受移动设备，此其时矣！

go.nmc.org / VIS

（马修·皮特里，《卫报》，2013 年 5 月 31 日）最近一项研究发现，纽约现代艺术博物馆 74％的游客都自带移动设备。位于伦敦的维多利亚和艾伯特博物馆在委托开展的一项研究透露，观众宁可使用个人的移动设备也不愿使用博物馆提供的设备。其中的原因包括自带设备的易用性和熟悉程度、卫生以及已经拥有的一种解说工具的便捷性。

教育是自带设备项目成功的关键

go.nmc.org / fierce

（大卫·韦尔登，菲尔斯调查公司，2013 年 10 月 10 日）许多组织要么采用正式的自带设备政策，要么容许非正式自带设备的使用，但在各种设备和网络之间的数据传输增加了泄密或受攻击的危险性。

因此，至关重要的是，每个员工要明白自带设备究竟是如何工作，以及他们的行为会如何导致潜在的风险。

"How-To"自助导览应用程序

go.nmc.org / selfg

（"官方白点博客"，2013年8月17日）这一"白点"框架旨在帮助博物馆、美术馆和公共场所建立和实施自助游应用程序，而无需昂贵的开发费用。参观者只要把自己的智能手机或平板电脑带来，就可以使用应用程序来浏览展品和收藏。

势在必行：在2013年年底之前，将有62%的公司允许自带设备

go.nmc.org / byodreport

（蒂娜·哈蒙德，《ZDNet》2013年2月4日）根据一项对《ZDNet》和《技术共和国》的1000名成员的全球性调查，超过44％的组织已经允许自带设备，另有18％的公司计划在2013年年底实施自带设备政策。报告全文披露参与该计划员工的百分比、最常用于工作的个人设备、关于安全措施的详细介绍以及硬件和服务计划的成本。

参观者对于在博物馆使用移动设备有什么想法和建议？

go.nmc.org / vam1

（安德鲁·刘易斯，维多利亚和艾伯特博物馆，2013年3月13日）研究者对伦敦的许多博物馆进行了一系列调查，以了解观众如何使用他们的移动设备，以及他们想获得什么样的博物馆内容和服务。在维多利亚和艾伯特博物馆的调查结果中，特别描述了一个手持智能手机的博物馆游客，他热衷于免费的无线网络，期望有根据用户兴趣、用户需要的角度设计的内容。

什么是自带设备？为什么它很重要？

go.nmc.org / byodtech

（迪安·埃文斯，《技术雷达》，2013年8月23日）IT消费化正迫使大小型企业和公司都转向效率最大化和降低安全风险的发展战略。这篇文章为那些想尝试新的IT管理方法的人概括了一些有效的自带设备政策及实施要点。

众 包
预期投入应用时间：1 年以内

众包，是指可用来发动群体贡献否则将湮没不闻的想法、信息或内容的一整套方法。它因为能高效弥补其他手段无法填补的空白而迅速发展。维基百科就是一个著名的案例，志愿者提供与其专业相关的信息和定义。众包利用的正是群体智慧，它发动成千上万的作者使知识不断精炼细化。对于博物馆学者来说，众包通常是研究人员吸取公众知识，填补有关社群或家族缺失的历史和其他细节，完成大规模任务，解决复杂问题的一种途径。博物馆机构认为，在为许多研究课题提供深度细节或编制大量文件材料的过程中，业余学者以及那些与重点研究对象如某事件、某物件或者某影像等同时代的人，其发挥的作用是极其重要的。众筹在很多方面与众包很相似。这是一种通过人际网络（通常是利用互联网资源）进行集资的方式。许多组织，尤其是处于创业初期的组织，会利用诸如 Kickstarter 等在线工具为新项目和新产品筹资。从灾难恢复到自由软件开发，众筹已经在为许多类型各异的活动提供支持而为大家所熟知。

概述

众包对博物馆和个人而言都是很有必要的。一些个人单独无法完成的工作，可以通过集合他人的思路和想法来完成。对于博物馆来说，在如"脸书""推特"等社交媒体平台它们更加容易同大范围的人群共享资源，获取投入。然而，众包的概念并不是新兴的，众多组织很久以前就曾请求其成员、粉丝和其他重点人群提供资源投入。也许已知最早的众包实例就是在没有网络支持的年代牛津英语词典公开征集词语的引用和例句。在 70 多年里，他们收到了超过 600 万份的反馈。

千禧年出现了许多靠众包生存的科技公司。Ancestry.com，23andMe 和其他一些公司利用不断增加的个人 DNA 测试来建立庞大的基因信息库，帮助测试者了解他们的家族历史。大型公众科学项目，如"康奈尔鸟类学实验室"和"北行"，依靠美国各地业余科学家提交的观察报告进行对鸟类和野生动物的日常研究并追踪其迁徙模式。博物馆也开始对文化遗址和文物进行类似的众包研究，他们希望从知情人士中收集信息。

众包不仅能帮助博物馆收集有关特定主题或文物的明确信息，同时也令观众和机构之间产生了更深层的联系，用创新的方式建立了信任和忠诚。德国哲学家瓦尔特·本雅明认为真正的艺术是艺术家和受众共同创造的，他因此而出名。众包充分体现了这个概念，它将受众变成了积极的参与者，因为他们的贡献最后成为了最终作品的一部分。

众筹是众包中发展最迅速的领域之一，特别是在 Kickstarter、Crowdfunder、Indiegogo 等类似网站的出现后，任何能上网的人都能成为慈善家去支持令人兴奋的新思路和新项目。博物馆、艺术家和各类用户通过在这些平台上支付一定的费用来开展筹资活动。如果资助者承诺资助的数额达到他们的筹款目标，该项目就会成功获得资金，而那些出资的人也就成为了这个项目成功故事的一部分。在许多情况下，这些人也会因为他们提供的支持得到一些回报，有可能是被资助项目的最终产品，也有可能是其他实惠。回报甚至是会分级别的，投资越多的人，得到的回报就越多。

由于博物馆本来面对的就是公众群体，因此非常适于利用各种众包的形式来吸纳观众，使观众成为它们所提供的体验的一部分。许多博物馆已经成功完成了小型和大型的众包项目，而这类举措一定还会继续增加。

与博物馆教育及传播的关联性

2012 年，众筹网站 Kickstarter 上为与艺术相关的项目筹集的资金第一次超过了美国国家艺术基金会所筹到的资金。这标志着融资的大环境发生了重大转变，表明了群众的力量从根本上改变了人们和博物馆之间的互动关系。无论是丰富展览内容，还是帮助学者们进行数据收集，普通民众的意见和行为越来越多地被博物馆所采纳和利用。

在充满挑战的经济环境下，为博物馆展览筹集资金变得更加困难，博物馆正在寻找其他方法来弥补展览预算的不足。众筹的概念并非新创，一小部分有钱的顾客在看到投资博物馆的好处后往往会走到一起，在经费上支持展览。真正新的是目前筹款所用的方法和出资人的类型。目前 Kickstarter 网站上的众筹活动为史密森研究所的弗里尔和赛克勒画廊的瑜伽展筹集资金，从 600 个有共同爱好的个人那里筹集到了 170000 美元。Kickstarter 预测这种类型的集资还会增加，因为他们在网站上创造了一个新的博物馆分类。

博物馆希望在个人对其投资的同时，

也希望用类似的方式让大众为他们的展览提供信息。它们展示用户生成的内容或让参观者为自己喜爱的艺术作品和艺术家投票。布鲁克林博物馆就因为使用了后一种策略而为人熟知。它们邀请当地的博物馆社区参观布鲁克林区的艺术家工作室，并为它们希望能收录在群展中的艺术家投票。

公众科学与众包以一种有趣的方式结合在一起，帮助科学博物馆兼备研究中心的功能。例如，Calbug 是一项对九个加利福尼亚自然历史博物馆藏有的超过一百万多件昆虫和蜘蛛展品进行众包和数字化的项目。参与者通过帮助转录数据使信息可以轻松被访问，并让研究人员了解生物多样性的变化，而获得徽章作为奖励。

库珀－休伊特博物馆利用众包来为大量没有元数据的藏品配备说明。他们的新藏品网站提供了通过内置的标记功能获取展品信息的服务。例如，在一件藏品的网页底部，有可以链接来自 Flickr、Instagram 个人照片或 SketchUp、Thingiverse 的 3D 模型的个人照片簿的标记按钮，这个功能可以把博物馆的藏品和用户内容连接起来。

随着游客越来越希望以更加私人的方式参与到博物馆事务，众包切实显示了合作和对话的力量。在众包被广泛使用的同时，博物馆仍需要克服接纳用户生成的内容和反馈的挑战。一个真正的众包项目需要博物馆放松对内容的掌控权，并欢迎偏离预期的想法，这样才能促进那种往往能带来创新的协同效应的生成。

下面是博物馆应用众包的例子：

> **展览和收藏** "编辑博物馆地图"是一个开放的数据项目，人们可以将布赖顿和霍伍市皇家展馆和博物馆的收藏藏品在网上虚拟地摆放在当地地图上，从而展示了城市和博物馆的关系。同时可以创建可以成为展品永久目录记录一部分的新数据：go.nmc.org/ MAPM。

> **市场营销和公共关系** 以创建"燕麦片网站"著称的马修·因曼利用社交媒体的力量分享他在 Indiegogo 众筹网站的筹资活动，成功筹集到了目标资金 850000 美元中的 520000 美元来修建一座特斯拉博物馆。他的集资活动的链接获得 12600 条 Twitter 分享，47000 个 Facebook 点赞，和 9700 个谷歌转发：go.nmc.org/tesla。

> **观众服务和无障碍辅助功能** 澳大利亚维多利亚博物馆使用了一个基于网络的开源项目，叫做"描述我"，旨在通过众包替换文本使视障人士能更容易在网上欣赏展品。每位志愿者被分配给一个图像，负责对这个图像写一段描述文字：go.nmc.org/ desau。

众包的应用实例

以下链接提供了在博物馆环境中应用众包的例子：

农业革新与历史资料

go.nmc.org/ament

史密森研究所下属的美国国家历史博物馆要求参观者参与到活动中来，即叙述改变美国农牧业历史的技术，并写下这些改变是如何影响他们生活的。这样做的目的是编制一个众包数字档案，这些档案为《美国企业展览》提供美国农业的状况。

艺术奖

go.nmc.org/ artpz

艺术奖是一年一度的历时19天以上的公开艺术比赛，在密歇根州的大急流城城区举行，任何年满18岁的人都可以提交他们的作品，并由公众来评判，荣获一等奖的参赛者有机会赢得20万美元奖金。这个大赛由艺术家和赞助商团体独立组织。

历史标记

go.nmc.org/ histp

历史标记（Historypin）是非营利性的"我们做什么我们就成为什么"和谷歌之间的合作项目。这个项目要求人们把自己的媒体资料——照片、信件和回忆——添加到一个公众资料档案，在这个档案中，历史文物被标记在某个位置上，并在谷歌地图上可以搜索得到。该网站还包含有一些藏品，用户可以通过照片探索某个特定的时期和地点。

玛丽娜·阿布拉莫维奇学院：创始人

go.nmc.org/abram

2013年7月，玛丽娜·阿布拉莫维奇学院启动了一场众筹活动，目的是筹集60万美元建造一座容纳被著名表演艺术家阿布拉莫维奇称为"不朽作品"的藏品楼，这些作品是艺术、科学、技术和精神的结合。该项目实现了预期目标，作为回报，凡捐献超过1美元的人可以获得阿布拉莫维奇本人的拥抱。

膨化枪

go.nmc.org/boom

食品和饮料博物馆通过Kickstarter完成了筹集80000美元的目标。这笔资金计划用于资助一种能把谷物变成燕麦早餐的膨化枪的研发。这种膨化枪连续三个星期六在曼哈顿进行展示。创始人戴夫·阿诺德是个厨师、电台主持人和餐馆老板，这是他第一次展览。

航天飞机"企业号"：开拓者

go.nmc.org/intrepid

纽约"无畏号"航母上的海空博物馆为"企业号"航天飞机创建了一个众包模

式的展品。博物馆要求公众将他们的航飞时刻照片上传到博物馆网站，或者以自己的标题发 Instagram 和 Twitter，这样博物馆就可以用这些内容同时创建实物和网络在线展览。

十大悬念

go.nmc.org / tenmo

"十大悬念"是为英国的塑料设计博物馆开发的项目，这是一个以游戏方式对该馆藏品中没有文献记录的事实进行核实的众包方法，要求参与者持续参与和合作。该模式可应用于其他情况中，例如识别绘画和照片中的人物和地点。

扩展阅读

若想了解更多有关众包方面的情况请参详下列文章和资源：

众包博物馆：大手笔捐助者、管理者的决定，以及个人艺术家可以被取代吗？

go.nmc.org/don

（保拉·牛顿，《玻璃轮胎》，2013年5月31日）本文为博物馆如何以众筹、群众投票和众包的方式获得更广泛的支持提供实例。作者认为，在开始众包活动之前，博物馆应考虑到如果集资目标不能实现所带来的影响，以及普通民众的意见如何以可控形式来影响艺术成果。

数字人文和众包：一次探索

go.nmc.org/anex

（劳拉·卡莱蒂、加布里埃拉·吉安纳奇、多米尼克·普莱斯、德里克·麦考利，《博物馆和网络》，2013年）随着文化机构正逐步尝试运用众包这种模式，本文作者利用对画廊、图书馆、档案馆、博物馆和教育机构的 36 种不同众包项目的网络调查，阐明了支持众包发展的不同做法。

哦，咔嚓！开放画廊授权的实验

go.nmc.org/ ohsnap

（尼娜·西门，《博物馆 2.0》，2013年 3 月 13 日）卡内基艺术博物馆的实验性摄影项目，"哦，咔嚓！你在卡内基博物馆拍的照片"允许实地和网络参观人士在场馆分享他们的作品。这篇文章描写了这个项目的优点，描述了博物馆是如何利用这个项目与参与者持续地进行对话的。

关于众包比赛中的"小花招"问题：从悉尼设计项目学到的

go.nmc.org /tricky

（米娅·里奇，《公开的作品》，2013年 5 月 27 日）本文介绍了从悉尼设计节期间举办的比赛获得的经验教训。该组织的众包活动被某些人视为一种从设计师那儿投机取巧地获取作品的不道德方式。

什么是众包？它是如何应用于外延项目的？

go.nmc.org /out

（《想法》，2013年2月19日）这个关于众包的概述把众包主题分为多个方面来解释，借以说明究竟众包是如何有助于机构的外延项目的。从云劳动到集体智慧，有多种不同的从社会获取支持的方式。

是的，Kickstarter 比国家艺术基金会为艺术家筹集了更多的钱。以下将说明为什么这并不令人惊讶。

go.nmc.org / RAI

（凯瑟琳·博伊尔，《华盛顿邮报》，2013年7月7日）Kickstarter 提供众筹平台，简化了由来已久的私人为艺术捐款的传统方式，为艺术项目筹集了6亿多美元。个人捐助者给艺术捐钱不是什么新鲜事——只有捐赠方式是全新的。

电子出版
预期投入应用时间：2~3 年

电子出版已经在消费行业站稳脚跟，目前又在重新定义印刷与数字、静态影像与视频、被动与互动内容之间的界限。从传统印刷到数字、网络、视频甚至互动内容，现代数字化工作流程几乎能完成内容的所有展示方式。电子出版几乎使用了所有潜在出版渠道，包括印刷、网络、视频、手机、平板电脑以及互动设备等。从发展伊始，电子出版就不仅仅是提高生产效率的手段，它还能利用多种媒体的内容来扩大产品的覆盖面。如果说，电子出版领域的第一次革命是让出版平台对每个人开放，那么下一阶段则是整合这些平台，以产生新组合、新类别的内容。诸如《在线学术目录计划》(OSCI)和《响应式设计》之类的新概念，将有助于实现内容的轻松存档并传送到任意设备上。

概况

电子出版的应用使博物馆可以设计生产出不需考虑最终版本的出版物，这样就实现了阅读内容在不同格式之间简便灵活地转换，为顾客提供各种各样的阅读选项。同时，每种阅读版本都是一次独特的经验，它的持续发展增添了出版物的特色多样性。现如今，电子出版物已经变得司空见惯，所有大型的杂志和期刊至少都会有一个电子版本。电子出版反映了不同形式的数字媒体向同一个单一的生产流线的汇集——这一概念在整个博物馆行业正在被广泛地采用。

自从 2011 年发表的《新媒体联盟地平线报告（博物馆版）》做了一次电子出版特刊之后，电子出版在过去的两年内发展迅猛。2012 年，皮尤研究中心（Pew Center）公布的一项研究表明，50% 的美国人通过在线获取新闻资讯，而 25 岁以下在线访问新闻的人数已攀升至 60%。《纽约时报》网站每月拥有 3000 多万独立访客，而其印刷版发行量已下降到每日 100 万份。此外，像

《大英百科全书》和《新闻周刊》一类的大型出版物已完全用电子刊物替代了纸质发行版。早在 30 多年前，媒体大亨鲁珀特·默多克（Rupert Murdoch）就预测过印刷出版时代的终结，现在，他的预言正在逐年成为现实。

响应式设计可以确保无论使用何种设备（台式电脑、笔记本电脑、智能手机或平板电脑），个人的阅读选择都能获得最佳的视觉体验。

在电子出版快速增长的过程中，出版行业面临着其内在的挑战——改变策略和工作流程，与此同时，科技本身仍在不断发展。出版公司首当其冲，自 2009 年以来，出版公司已精简了生产—制造—行销的工作流程。在电子出版产生之前，还没有那么多的移动应用，当时的应用本身也很容易理解，出版就是印刷、文字以及图片。视频和多媒体曾是明显不同的形式，但是现在很难做这样的区分了——越来越多的最终出版物都包括了这些不同形式的内容，那些重要报纸、杂志和网站亦是如此。

如今许多博物馆的内容和市场团队都把自己看成媒体公司，专注于推出那些呈现格式覆盖范围最广的内容。新兴格式的出现使出版方能够为同一作品制作不同版本——比如附有作者采访或光面插图的扩展版——以适应特定的读者群。只需采集一次内容，就可以将其应用到多种潜在格式上。此外，移动应用软件自身也已然成为出版物。博物馆使用移动应用软件发布藏品的照片、视频和对艺术家的采访——让人们在更深的层面与电子材料进行互动。

2013 年电子出版发展的新领域是其新的设计方式和方法。例如响应式设计，即在任何设备上（台式电脑、笔记本电脑、智能手机或平板电脑）个人的阅读选择都能获得最佳的视觉体验。响应式设计使导航迅速适应显示器的尺寸和形状，自动调整内容的大小，流畅地适用于当前的浏览器和屏幕尺寸。

与博物馆教育及传播的关联性

最近的发展，尤其是《在线学术目录计划》(OSCI) 的实施阶段的发展，使公开共享的资料剧增，并且博物馆及其工作人员也开始更多地采用电子出版策略。虽然大型博物馆已有许多电子出版物目录和移动应用软件，但缺乏可行性商业模式，使其电子出版物的发展未能广泛投入应用。

《盖蒂的在线学术目录计划》始于 2008 年，旨在通过在网络上传播学术研究去增加藏品访问量。当时，博物馆才刚刚开始理解这个新媒体的潜力。五年后，参与到该项目的九个博物馆都在积极尝试着不同形式的网络出版，并与其他更多博物馆共享研究成果。新的资源和工作流程以及《在线学术目录计划》建立的正式平台工具包，都引进了一种新的思维方式，即博物馆的目录制作、内容管理和数字化战略。芝加哥艺术馆的一些学者，之前一直不愿去接触电子出版物，现如今却把《在线学术目录计划》工具包作为极具价值的研究工具。

自古以来，出版博物馆刊物都是昂贵的，因为印刷和版权成本过高，但随着出版物的数字化，图像权限能更轻松地从国家美术馆、大英博物馆、阿姆斯特丹国立博物馆等这些机构获取。与此同时，这些博物馆中原本秘不示人的部分藏品现在访问量大量增加，这对研究更加有利。

同时，传统出版是一个耗时和封闭的过程，过程中单个部门内的活动基本上都是"孤立的"。对工作流程进行了深思熟虑之后，多个部门开始相互协作，共同推动网络、移动、印刷和展馆内的体验平行发展。更戏剧性的转变是，随着人们越来越习惯使用 Instagram 和 tumblr 的免费在线出版物，博物馆工作人员和理事会的态度悄然发生了变化，他们对科技应用于博物馆更加包容了。

随着电子出版物自身功能的增多，与以往相比，残疾人也可以欣赏到更多的艺术品。乌姆劳夫雕塑花园博物馆自 1991 年开始就为来自德州学校的盲人学生提供"触摸式参观"，最近通过 iPad 上的大号字资料来增强这种"触摸式参观"。iBooks Author 的使用，使博物馆可以在 iBook 上为选定的艺术品进行口头描述，重点介绍了七件雕塑，并为盲人和低视力的游客进行公园路线导航。此外，由于这种形式的出版物可以在平板电脑上访问，可调节亮度的阅读材料使具备中等中心视力的观众能够更加轻松快速地进行阅读。

电子出版不仅包含了越来越多的数字格式和媒体，而且其流程能够很容易为同一故事制作多种版本，无论是出于学术本质的需要，还是为了针对更广泛的读者的鉴赏能力。这一技术如此快速的发展，使人们认为电子出版并不是一套产品，而是作为一种新的、不同的方式在传递资源。由于电子出版的灵活性，越来越多的博物馆正在采用电子出版模式，盖因其只需要创建一次，就可以在多处出版。

以下是电子出版在博物馆的一些应用：

> 保护　电子博物馆收藏目录可以比之前印刷版本包含更多有关保护方面的文献资料。旧金山现代艺术博物馆劳森伯格的研究项目为学术研究和文献资

料提供了全球范围内的访问可能，这些学术研究和文献资料包括旧金山现代艺术博物馆永久藏品中的罗伯特·劳森伯格画作背后的故事以及与劳森伯格的艺术作品相关的保护研究报告和视频资料（go.nmc.org/rau）。

> **展览和藏品** 波士顿艺术博物馆通过 iPad 电子书，让他们的乐器藏品变得鲜活起来。用户可以看到和听到由音乐家演奏的 100 种乐器的视频剪辑和音频样本，这些全部是选自博物馆收藏的 1100 种乐器，包括从古希腊的号角到南印度的琵琶，再到美国的夏威夷钢棒吉他（go.nmc.org/musical）。

> **营销和公共关系** 加州奥克兰博物馆（OMCA）提供一个免费的数字杂志应用程序，定期更新展览预告和艺术家、社会活动家的相关视频。除了博物馆特有的媒体，OMCA 的应用程序还提供了当地景点和公园的交互式地图，以及来自协作博物馆的藏品的幕后图像信息（go.nmc.org/omca）。

电子出版的实际应用

以下链接提供了电子出版在博物馆的一些应用实例

《催化剂杂志》

go.nmc.org/denmus

丹佛自然与科学博物馆向其观众免费提供双月在线出版物《催化剂杂志》。该电子杂志内容包括关于事件、活动和展览的相关信息。可通过 Facebook，Twitter，Pinterest 优化链接共享。

学院艺术协会

go.nmc.org/caa

安德鲁·W. 梅隆基金会正在赞助学院艺术协会制定、发布并推广在艺术品的创作和管理以及视觉艺术的学术出版方面版权正当使用的规范。这将帮助艺术家和艺术史学家获得授权以电子或纸质的形式复制艺术品。

达拉斯网站

go.nmc.org/dmg

达拉斯艺术博物馆的数字出版物《达拉斯场所：发展中的艺术场景，从战后至今》，通过影像、论文和学术作品追溯了在达拉斯七个城区中当代艺术场景的发展历程。该出版物探索了在北德州自 20 世纪 50 年代中期兴起的 150 多种商业画廊和非营利组织。

期刊索引

go.nmc.org/harvart

今年早些时候，哈佛大学艺术博物馆推出了与《期刊索引》对应的数字版，包括关于藏品的文章与访谈资料。网站上包含与博物馆工作人员互动的机会，如"向馆长提问活动日"窗口可以让馆长们通过 Twitter 来回答公众提出的问题。

大都会艺术博物馆出版物

go.nmc.org/metro

纽约大都会艺术博物馆发布了一项名为"大都会出版物荟萃"的新项目，该项目可以提供过去五十年内的书籍、公告和期刊，还附加 375 本免费艺术书籍和目录。当前市场上的图书也可以通过该网站预览，而绝版书籍则可通过按需印刷去获取。

戏剧艺术在英国

go.nmc.org/publ

维多利亚和艾伯特博物馆推出的"百部话剧展现现代英国戏剧艺术"iPad 应用程序，引导观众获取英国 60 年演艺历史的相关照片、原始脚本内容摘要和音频剪辑。

扩展阅读

如想了解更多有关电子出版方面的内容，建议参详以下文章和资源。

从无到有创建传播技术战略（视频）

go.nmc.org/ittt

（科文·斯密斯，《新媒体联盟》，2013年 10 月 1 日）作为一位博物馆技术人员，他解释了如何使用免费的博物馆联合工具"If This Then That"为电子出版物添加智能交互功能，同时又能自我维持。

一次创建，多处出版——博物馆收藏品内容的再利用

go.nmc.org/cope

（保罗·罗威，《藏品及其关联》，2013年 6 月 7 日）作为博物馆软件公司的开发人员，他把内容管理的策略描述为"一次创建，多处出版"，如今全国公共广播电台正在实行该策略。罗威把这一策略应用于博物馆世界，旨在帮助各机构在网上对藏品信息进行再利用。

未来就是现在："盖蒂之声"回顾《在线学术目录计划》并展望博物馆数字出版的未来

go.nmc.org/neely

（莉斯·尼利，《博物馆数字出版维基网志》，2013 年 8 月 14 日）在这篇文章中，芝加哥艺术馆的数字信息和访问主任，突出强调数字出版的重要性，其灵感源于盖蒂基金会的安妮·赫尔姆茨克的观点。她认为必须成立一个数字化学术出版商的社团，通过会议互相分享经验或与研发者合作，共享集体知识，从而推进电子出版的发展。

精心策划电子出版的力量：印第安纳波利斯艺术博物馆（IMA）的石墨艺术品展

go.nmc.org/graph

（格雷格·阿尔伯斯，《数字出版》，

2013年4月4日）印第安纳波利斯艺术博物馆石墨艺术品展的数字展品目录有三大特色：目录上方设有导览链接；以实体展览照片进行数字导览；读者可以在数字展品目录里轻松地观看视频。

多媒体创作平台的崛起

go.nmc.org/multi

（里奇·西弗纳,《出版人周刊》，2013年2月1日）因为有了各种多媒体创作工具，同时越来越多的出版商开始热衷于电子读物的出版。现在，公司和各种组织生产、制作数字出版物越来越容易了。这些数字出版物包括音频、视频、图像、动画和3D模型。本文作者对包括iBooks Author、VooK和Inkling等在内的新一代媒体出版商进行了研究并对这些公司开发利用电子出版这一新兴市场的方法进行了评估。

位基服务
预期投入应用时间：2~3 年

位基服务（简称 LBS）根据用户所处地理位置向其提供量身定制的动态信息。这些信息通常会发送至移动设备；蜂窝塔定位信息会根据 GPS 数据进行调整以保证对移动设备的定位高度精准。新技术可以将精准的定位服务扩展至建筑物内部和室内空间。目前常见的位基服务有：广告、新闻、社交以及其他类似的服务。在商业领域，通过分析用户兴趣方面的数据，并利用定位技术使用户在其所处位置做出相应购买行为，这已然成为商家促销的常见手法。位基服务的下一发展阶段，也是最引人注目的，就是室内地理定位。室内定位可以为访客提供与其在建筑内的确切位置相符的具体信息。这些信息或服务都根据访客所处的位置进行了精确调整。新技术定位的不只是访客的平面位置，还包括其在 3D 立体空间所处的位置。新定位技术甚至可以识别建筑物的不同楼层。

概述

位基服务通过无线网络或移动网络精确定位某一物体或个人的物理位置。位基服务之所以引人关注是因为它能利用用户的位置信息向用户提供各种服务，比如，通过移动应用程序为用户规划最佳旅行线路，向用户推荐值得一看的博物馆和展览等。由于智能手机和平板电脑本身就带有定位系统和各式传感器，位基服务可以确保用户和其所处位置之间流畅的通信流，从而使大量的移动服务和应用成为可能。

位基服务并不是一个全新的领域，但人们对它却越来越感兴趣，原因就在于位基服务和人们已经普遍使用的工具（特别是社交网络）无缝地结合在了一起。过去几年，博物馆一直热衷于创造性地利用社交媒体，所以自然也就会对位基技术善加利用。

如今，用户新注册某个社交网络（如

Instagram 或 Facebook）时，马上就会收到这样一条确认信息，询问用户是否允许该平台获取其当前的地理位置。事实上，一些社交网络的整个经营都是建立在用户位置信息基础之上的。美国社交定位网站 FourSquare 就是一个很好的例子。过去几年里，FourSquare 已经成为社交媒体圈里运行时间最久的网站之一。FourSquare 对那些通过移动设备检入位置信息的用户进行奖励。各个商家，包括博物馆，也纷纷受到这种虚拟交换的启示，开始给那些通过各种社交网络检入、标记、确认自己所处位置的用户一些折扣或特别优惠。位基服务横跨数字领域和实体领域，促成了两大领域前所未有的无缝对接。

无论在室内或室外，当位基服务同大数据、人们的习惯及行动轨迹的分析结合起来，就能超越大小或空间的概念，转而关注依据用户的兴趣为用户提供量身定制信息的方法。位基服务的未来发展方向不再是开发能够定位个人位置的设备，而是主动为用户推送有用的信息。也就是说，如果用户之前去过某些博物馆，那么他/她的智能手机就能根据已保存的相关参observing信息为其今后参观提供建议。

苹果公司最近收购了两家智能定位公司，Locationary 和 WiFiSLAM。这两家创业公司专业从事 GPS 室内定位和众包地理位置数据库的开发。苹果的收购反映出位基服务发展的一个新方向，预示了其在大型博物馆广阔的应用前景。位基服务现在致力于帮助人们更好地掌握周边环境信息，甚至能够让人们亲身参与到室内和室外地图的绘制中来。

与博物馆教育及传播的关联性

位基服务可以为博物馆参观者提供个性化的教育体验。最近，博物馆已经开始在公共区域提供免费无线网络，这给那些自带移动设备的顾客带来了便利。通过 WiFi 三角测量在移动设备上为参观者提供指路服务和数字讲解材料是位基服务最新进展的核心，同时，在为参观者提供便利的个性化参观体验方面，位基服务仍有很大的发展空间。

位基服务可以为博物馆参观者提供便利的个性化教育体验。

尽管人们现在还在对各种各样的室内定位系统进行研究，例如蓝牙信号定位、室内 LED 定位、无线射频识别定位，但室内定位的核心策略还是利用 WiFi 三角测量将位基服务信息直接传输到用户的手持移动设备上。在芝加哥艺术馆（AIC），稳定的网络连接和室内定位服务让游客得以以一种全新的方式来参观这个有着 150 年历史的古老博物馆。为了更好地实现教育目的，过去几年里，芝加哥艺术馆对展馆进行了改造，几乎所有的公共区域都安装了无线网络。通过仔细规划无线网络接入点，博物馆能够在方圆近10米的范围内测量出游客的具体位置，并引导他们去参观配有相应电子资源的精选艺术品。

在未来两到三年内，位基服务在社交维度的应用必将在博物馆领域大幅扩大。社交传媒和实体空间早前依靠FourSquare和Yelp这样的移动应用程序相互作用，最近则通过众包地理位置应用Locationary和众包地图应用Waze相互影响。社交传媒和实体空间之间的相互作用使个人能够基于物理位置在社交网络上建立社区。例如，在美国迪科尔多瓦雕塑公园和博物馆，艺术家哈尔西·勃艮（Halsey Burgund）在她的声音类应用Scapes上使用了雕塑公园的地理位置。通过Roundware这样一个可以感应地理位置的音频平台，博物馆的参观者可以一边使用导航功能，一边在移动设备上欣赏不同乐器演奏出来的声音。同时，博物馆还鼓励参观者对自己欣赏艺术品的感悟进行录音或收听其他游客的欣赏感悟录音。

博物馆在网络空间和实体空间都占有重要地位。凭借日益成熟的个人位置定位技术，博物馆让网络空间和实体空间之间的互动变得比以往任何时候都更有意义。借助地理围栏技术，博物馆的网站能够知晓参观者的具体位置，并把与该位置相关的信息推送给参观者。例如，如果参观者就在博物馆入口处附近，博物馆网站就会向参观者的移动设备发送有关博物馆开放时间和票价的信息；如果参观者正在驻足欣赏某一件艺术品，网站就会给他（她）发送这件馆藏艺术品的相关信息。

尽管目前有很多位基服务项目已在进行中，但这项技术还是放在了预期投入应用的中期阶段里，主要还是因为对博物馆进行技术升级改造花费巨大，并且目前室内定位的精准度也有待提高。

位基服务在博物馆领域的具体应用包括以下方面：

> 展览与藏品　铁姆肯艺术馆推出了一款手机应用程序试验版，该应用程序能根据参观者在馆内的位置为其提供艺术品的相关信息。每件艺术品都配有定位设备，通过向参观者的智能手机和平板电脑发送低功率无线电信号确定参观者的位置，并发送相关信息给参观者。参见：go.nmc.org/timken。

> 营销与通讯　现在FourSquare已整合进Instagram照片共享应用，博物馆可以借助FourSquare，通过Instagram用户在应用平台上分享的有地理标记的照片收集位置信息。通过分析参观者的行为，博物馆可以深入了解某一展览或活动最受欢迎的部分是什么。参见：go.nmc.org/nitro。

> 观众服务与博物馆的无障碍服务加拿大皇家卑诗省博物馆与WiFarer公司合

作推出了一款应用程序，该应用通过参观者位置定位地图帮助参观者找到自己喜欢的艺术品和藏品，从而实现个性化的参观。基于位置的内容为每件展品增加了更深层的互动。参见：go.nmc.org/rbc。

位基服务的应用实例

下列链接为博物馆及其他场景中的位基服务实例：

ByteLight

go.nmc.org/byte

马萨诸塞州 ByteLight 公司的 LED 灯泡使用肉眼不可见的信号作用于波士顿科学博物馆观众携带的移动设备的相机上，并借此向游客发送具体定位信息。

弗恩班克博物馆应用程序

go.nmc.org/fer

在亚特兰大的弗恩班克自然历史博物馆，观众一旦进入馆内，其定位应用程序马上就追踪观众位置以发送包括音频、视频、触屏互动、动画、速写活动，以及回答问题在内的信息，同时也鼓励观众通过社会媒体平台分享他们的经历。

芝加哥艺术馆室内 GPS

go.nmc.org/indo

芝加哥艺术馆使用一种由默里迪恩公司提供支持的室内 GPS 定位系统带领观众沿着按照时机、主题、藏品和时间来定制的线路进行参观。每条路线展示了 6~10 件艺术品，包括展品说明和逐项导航。

英国皇家植物园 GPS 应用程序

go.nmc.org/kew

英国皇家植物园开发了一个安卓应用程序，该应用程序使用 GPS 和 WiFi 技术为游客寻路和解说提供了新方法。该应用程序指引游客在 1.21 平方千米的户外空间和三个玻璃温室进行游览，并向游客提供关于周围植物树木的互动媒体信息。

公园掌中游应用程序

go.nmc.org/chal

自然公园网络公司的"公园掌中游"应用程序邀请用户进行"地理挑战游"，在以后尽可能多的游览加利福尼亚州公园和休闲游乐区，并使用有全球定位系统功能的应用程序标出每次出行路线图。参与者通过游览公园和休闲游乐区获得积分，游览较近的公园可获得 5 分，而较远的地点可获得 20 分。

维基媒体的 Nearby

go.nmc.org/nearby

维基媒体基金会推出一个新的 Nearby 页面同其移动站点协同运行，该页面根据用户位置显示词条。同时，维基媒体的编辑可以轻松地为需要图片的词条上传照片或更新就近话题的词条。

扩展阅读

如想了解更多的位基服务，请参见下列文章和资料：

iBeacon 在棒球场的率先使用暗示了苹果的位基服务革命

go.nmc.org/ibe

（罗杰·程，*CNet*，2013 年 9 月 28 日）iOS7 的一个新功能 iBeacon，改善了 iPhone 的位基服务功能。近期 MLB.com 在花旗棒球场检验了其性能，当游客进入球场时，他们会收到一条欢迎短信和优惠折扣。

将历史做成应用程序（幻影）

go.nmc.org/hist

（罗德里·马尔斯顿，《ioL 旅游》，2013 年 8 月 15 日）"约克市全息游览"是由约克市议会支持的应用程序，当游客到达某处，它显示出身着剧装的演员扮演成历史人物介绍该地点历史的全息演示。文章作者描述了使用该应用程序的经历以及在未来的发展趋势——当用户拥有智能眼镜或其他可佩戴装置，它的功能将会得到更大的发挥。

博物馆环境下的位基指引服务：部署问题和推荐建设方案

go.nmc.org/guid

（尼古劳斯·康斯坦丁诺等人，《学术教育》，2013 年 10 月 1 日）此文分析了博物馆安装对环境触发做出回应的位基指引服务需达到的部署要求。该服务建在开放、模块化的平台上，利用可重复使用的零部件，并有支持不同类型设备的界面，包括可以搭载 Java 和蓝牙的智能手机。

地图绘制和位基地理服务

go.nmc.org/geo

[（Yu-Tzu Chiu,《IEEE 综览杂志》，2012 年 11 月 20 日）]ST 微电子有限公司和 CSR 半导体公司的工程师改良了谷歌 Nexus One 智能手机，在其内安装了室内导航模块，可供台北当代艺术馆的游客使用。当游客靠近一个展项，设备上就会弹出相应的图标，游客可以点击图标获取更多信息。

初创公司 Estimote 价廉的感应器可以创造为日常生活所用的操作系统

go.nmc.org/star

（凯尔·凡赫穆特,《连线杂志》，2013 年 8 月 7 日）Estimote 公司试图利用价廉、低能耗的传感器网络创立一个应用于实体世界的操作系统。创立者设想一个无缝的位置识别功能，带给人们与现实地点（包括从公园到停车场）紧密整合的互动和体验。

为什么 WiFi 网络是位基移动设备的未来

go.nmc.org/meri

（尼克·法里纳,nfarina.com，2013 年 5 月）默里迪恩公司帮助美国自然历史博物馆建立"美国自然历史博物馆探索者"手机应用程序，它利用设备的 WiFi 信号确定游客在馆内的位置。作者相信 WiFi 是位基服务发展的关键，尤其在室内利用 GPS 定位方面。

自然用户界面
预期投入应用时间：4~5 年

目前，完全通过运用自然动作和手势与新型设备进行交互已经很常见了。iPad、iPhone、iPod Touch、Xbox Kinect、Nintendo Wii、新型智能电视以及其他越来越多的设备都建立在自然用户界面的基础上。它们接受轻触、滑动和其他触摸类型的输入方式，手势及手臂动作，身体动作，并且逐渐地开始接受自然语言。这些是最先出现的一批能够识别、读懂肢体语言并将其作为指令的设备。新技术继续在扩展这些功能，甚至能通过语音和脸部微表情来识别用户的情绪状态。有一类新的屏幕技术已经初具雏形，它们可以传输高精细的质地感受，提供相当自然的触觉反馈。2013 年，自然用户界面的亮点在于：出现了能够识别手势、面部表情以及表情细微差别的高保真系统，以及手势感知技术与语音识别和新型触感反馈（比如电振动）的融合。通过这些新技术，用户可以自然地通过手势、表情和语音与设备进行互动，表达自己的意图。

概述

尽管大规模普及自然用户界面要追溯到 2007 年 iPhone 手机及其触摸屏的上市，但在当时，这项技术本身并非原创。围绕超越命令行界面（CLI）和图形用户界面（GUI）的界面开发讨论始于 20 世纪七八十年代，当时被称为可携带计算机之父的史蒂夫·曼恩开始了人机交互实验。自然用户界面(NUI)的思想就始于他的研究，随后其他科学家和设计师不断将这一创新应用到新技术中。也许与其他的学习环境相比，博物馆本身就具有将大规模自然用户界面技术整合到展品和藏品中的优势。

人在通过自然用户界面与计算机进行交互时并不经常关注它的框架，因为他们的手势无缝地影响着他们的体验，这种模拟现实世界中的体验远远超出基于诸多命令和图形等象征手段的界面所能带来的感受。这一创新的吸引力在于博物馆观众可以获得不同模式呈现出来的，但是又不同于传统界面那样有距离感的信息体验。换言之，再没有什么可以阻挡用户和信息之间的交流了，参观者有机会真正与艺术品互动了。

在博物馆领域，自然用户界面对学习者产生了深远的影响。例如，孩子们在操作多点触控界面时，可以自然而然地适应这种机制，这为使用智能手机、平板电脑和微软 Kinect 等工具进行学习提供了更多的支持。自然用户界面也迎合了盲聋人群和自闭症患者、阅读障碍或其他残疾人群的需求，使这些人群更容易地通过触摸、语音和其他手势进行交流和学习。

触摸屏和视频运动传感器产品已经流行多年，其中包括任天堂的 Wii 和微软的 Kinect，它们一直是实现完全自然互动道路上的关键基准。电动震是实现真实连接的下一步。这一科技最早发明于 1954 年，指的是当手指划过覆盖有绝缘层导电表面时，形成的静电产生可感的触感和质感的过程。将这一电感应触觉应用于移动设备预示着触屏技术的下一个发展方向，为触摸到所看到的博物馆艺术品提供了潜在的可能性。

芬兰公司 Senseg 处于将这种触觉技术应用于智能手机和平板电脑的最前沿。迪斯尼研究院也在探索电震动技术。Senseg 的电震动技术可以应用于任何触摸界面去制造出所谓的"触感屏幕"，用户可以感受到屏幕上的质感。"触感屏幕"对博物馆来说是一个特别令人兴奋的技术，未来的"触感屏幕"增强设备可以提供与教育内容深度互动的多种可能性，通过它还可以为身残和智障人士提供无障碍服务。

语音翻译也增加了对自然用户界面的关注度。在移动设备的使用中，经常可以看到人们使用声控虚拟助手。接下来包括自动翻译引擎这一新技术，微软工程师演示了可以合成一个人的声音到另一种语言中的软件，比如从英语到汉语。这些机器学习技术的进步向我们展示了人与人之间以及人与学习内容之间可以更高效连接的世界。

与博物馆教育及传播的关联性

自然用户界面使技术变得显而易见，并改变了博物馆展览和藏品的呈现方式以及参观者与博物馆及其藏品的互动方式。博物馆观众历来都有触摸和操作藏品的欲望，尽管保护与修护问题可能会限制与原件藏品的互动，但是如今应用自然用户界面技术可以通过参观者的体验性接触或者空间旋转展品来弥补这一遗憾。随着新的用户界面逐渐成为主流，博物馆有机会使用这些先进技术来创造出全新的传播和展示方式。

美国克利夫兰艺术博物馆 12 米的藏品墙，是美国最大的多点触摸屏，它使得参观者可以用完全不同的方式与博物馆馆藏进行互动的前沿。多点触控技术让参观者移动、选择和整理多媒体资源，用非常直观的方式进行开放式的探索。此藏品墙在博物馆空间内对之进行了展示，其规模前所未见。

除了多点触控技术外，动作感应输入设备从根本上改变了博物馆参观者与藏品的互动方式。在新墨西哥艺术馆，牵线木偶曾被认为太脆弱不适于展出，但现在它们被赋予了新的生命。从博物馆的收藏中选出部分木偶，并创建数字化的替代品后，来自新墨西哥高地大学的学生通过使用 Kinect，让观众使用自然的手势来了解这些展品是如何活动的，这也是几十年来的首次。

随着艺术家们进一步扩展这一新工具的应用范围，以营造一种大规模的浸入式环境，自然用户界面的另一个方面已开始应用于画廊展示。2013 年夏天，现代艺术博物馆展出了一个"雨室"，这一艺术装置可以让参观者通过在房间内移动以防止模拟雨滴落在身上，这种房间内装备有传感器来识别物体和运动的存在。

新兴的传感技术，如迪斯尼研究院牵头的电震动项目，可以通过数字化手段来了解物体丰富的空间维度，而不必担心破坏脆弱的物体，从而开辟了一个全新的传播世界。通过手指与屏幕之间的摩擦力模拟边缘、突出物和隆起，参观者将能够以一种全新的方式体验到颜料厚涂的梵高作品。

从《新媒体联盟地平线报告（2012 博物馆版）》第一次刊登了此技术（当时也把它放在了预期投入应用的远期阶段内）以来，博物馆内探究式学习的趋势正在稳步发展。尽管进行了许多实验，自然用户界面仍然需要四五年的发展，因为鲜有博物馆自身具备开发这种技术用于教育目的的技能。尽管如此，特别展览的举办不仅为博物馆积累了更多的设备，同时也积累了以更富想象力的方式使用自然用户界面所需的专业知识，自然用户界面技术前景一片光明。

自然用户界面在博物馆和其他情景中的应用举例如下：

> 展览和收藏　　在卢浮宫《安地诺面纱》展览中使用微软 Kinect 的手势传感器技术，使参观者可以与一个古董手工艺品互动。古希腊挂毯脆弱娇贵且很难进行讲解，现在参观者可以通过数字形式对其接触：go.nmc.org/louvre。

> 市场及公共关系　　达拉斯的儿科医学中心有一个互动的捐赠荣誉墙，在那里每个气泡都展示了一个捐赠者的名字，用

户可以用手势进行操作：go.nmc.org/dono。

> **观众服务和无障碍辅助功能** 曼彻斯特博物馆开发出一种技术，利用一种叫做 Probos 触觉装置，可以让盲人和弱视参观者触摸展品的数字模型。参观者坐在设备面前，其配有一块屏幕，通过机械手臂与一个触控笔相连，屏幕会显示一个物体的 3D 模型，如罐子、骨头或雕像：go.nmc.org/fee。

自然用户界面的实践案例

下面的链接是自然用户界面在博物馆和其他场馆中的实例：

3D 动漫鸟和手势识别
go.nmc.org/nati

联域有限公司用 Kinect 体感传感器为《国家地理》杂志"天堂鸟"展览制作了"舞蹈，舞蹈的演化"游戏。玩家可以通过运动控制一个虚拟的 3D 鸟进行真正的求偶舞蹈仪式。

3D 制作的鲍曼木偶
go.nmc.org/mari

高地大学的学生在用 Kinect 为创造新墨西哥艺术馆收藏的大约 75 个古斯塔夫·鲍曼木偶的 3D 展示。用户将通过手势来操纵木偶，并且 3D 木偶模型也将能在博物馆的在线数据库中获取。

"夜行动物的感官"展览
go.nmc.org/natu

在罗马尼亚自然科学博物馆展出的"夜行动物的感官"展览向参观者展示了动物如何在夜间频繁活动。展览由各种尺寸的屏幕组成，触摸时便展现出动物所处的生活环境、捕猎习惯以及它们如何在黑暗中活动。

"商店生活"展项
go.nmc.org / shoplife

在美国纽约市，移民公寓博物馆的"商店生活"展项是一个 7.62 米长的互动桌面，为观众提供了了解从 19 世纪 60 年代到 20 世纪 70 年代 3 个移民商业场景的机会。故事通过图片、视频和音频在观众之间进行分享。

"体育馆"展项
go.nmc.org/pero

佩罗博物馆"体育馆"展项邀请观众抛出一个快球，踢个足球或来个侧手翻。与此同时，该展项通过高速相机捕捉这些动作，以便于观众回顾自己的动作去了解运动方面的知识以及身体姿势如何影响速度和运动科学的其他因素。

"思考"展项
go.nmc.org / thinkex

在 2.1 米的交互式触摸屏媒体介质的帮助下，涅克塔迪博物馆展出的"思考"展项以互动的方式，让访客来回顾技术革新的历史。展品的技术支持由 IBM 提供。

"声音宇宙"展项

go.nmc.org/univ

"声音宇宙"展项在伦敦科学博物馆展出，它整合了视频室、乐器、三维运动传感器隔间，创造出了一个身临其境的体验，参观者可以从中了解如何才能成为一名音乐家或爱乐乐团指挥。

"戴多顶帽子"（视频）

go.nmc.org/hats

在马萨诸塞州的皮博迪博物馆，被称为"戴多顶帽子"的互动站鼓励游客探索历代帽子的设计。参观者通过使用触摸屏来捕捉自己的照片，滚动查看各种帽子，直到他们找到喜欢的。然后，他们可以发送电子邮件保存或打印出自己带虚拟帽子的照片。

扩展阅读

如果您想了解更多关于自然用户界面技术的内容，请参阅以下文章和资源：

从取得突破性创新的博物馆获得的五点用户界面设计方面的经验

go.nmc.org/bre

（克利夫·邝，《快速公司》杂志，2013 年 3 月 6 日）克利夫兰艺术博物馆重新开放了一系列经过改造的画廊，让参与者与艺术互动，在这个过程中重点突出展品内容，而不是让新技术占了上风。例如，一个虚拟的画架放置在一幅杰克逊·波洛克的画作前，配备近似波洛克自己的作画工具，让观众可以创作自己的滴画法画作并与真迹进行比较。

位于赫尔辛基的初创公司 Senseg 创造出有触感的触摸屏

go.nmc.org / helsin

（斯蒂芬·凯利，《连线》杂志，2013 年 4 月 11 日）芬兰公司 Senseg 已经生产出一种超薄耐久材料，用超低电流制造出一种吸力，让用户感受到纹理、边缘和振动。他们计划为智能手机和平板电脑原型产品打造"有触感"的用户界面。

Leap Motion：应用程序下载量 3 周内达到 100 万

go.nmc.org / leapmo

（约翰·科特西尔，《摆平风险》，2013 年 8 月 12 日）Leap Motion 创造出一台无键盘的电脑控制器，比微软 Kinect 精准 200 倍，允许用户用隔空手势控制他们的电脑。该软件推出三周后，Leap Motion 应用程序的下载量超过 100 万次，其软件开发工具包下载量也超过 25000 次。

更人性化的照明解决方案

go.nmc.org/light

（PSFK 网站，2013 年 9 月 22 日）在伦

敦的里士满公园安装了LumiMotion照明系统，它能够探测到一个人在夜间接近灯柱，并相应地增加亮度。人经过灯柱后，灯光亮度会减小以节省能源。

医学博物馆筹集资金创建触摸屏墙以及其他高科技超值服务

go.nmc.org / doyle

（丽兹·希夫曼，《芝加哥DNA信息》，2013年4月8日）一位计算机科学家兼博物馆专家正在国家健康与医学博物馆进行没有围墙的博物馆的原型设计，为在芝加哥建设一个附属的卫星博物馆提供支持。对于这一全新的展馆，他设想构建可根据展陈或重大活动进行定制的从地面到天花板的交互式屏幕。

迪士尼新技术可在完全平滑的触摸屏上添加纹理

go.nmc.org/distech

（公共广播公司，2013年10月7日）美国匹兹堡的迪斯尼的研究人员已将电震动应用于平滑的触摸屏来制造质感，模仿突起、凹陷和其他三维体验。新技术还充分利用通过拉伸指尖皮肤来让大脑感知突起的研究。

保护与修护技术
预期投入应用时间：4~5 年

博物馆自诞生以来，其使命就是保护与修护我们共同的文化遗产。保护是指保护重要的物品、工艺品和文档；修护是指尽可能维持物品的原始形态。不管是保护还是修护，都要保证其过程是可逆的。这样，我们的后代可以对其进行复原或修正。随着技术的发展，档案管理者和修复师在这两方面不断面临新的挑战。数码文件有时与历史文物一样脆弱，需要细心保管，而不断变革的技术使这些数字产品的留存处于极大危险之中。基于时间的文化作品令保护工作更为复杂，因为这类作品还需考虑艺术家的意图、情境或动态效果等因素。如何在理解与保护数字媒体的体验方式和意图的同时还保持文化认同的完整性，这种过程还需要考虑很多因素，诸如保护准则、法律协议、机械/数字材料的可用性以及历史学知识等。长期以来，大型博物馆仅需聘用文物保护专家，而现在它们还需要聘用一些新的专业技术人员，这些新的专技人员必须懂得数字媒体和时基媒体，不仅可以从外观方面，而且可以更多地从艺术、文化、工程、电子等多学科视角应对保护和修复挑战。

概述

虽然保护和修护两词通常可以交替使用（注：英文里两个词比较相近），但它两者的目的是截然不同的；保护是为了保护和/或延缓文物的自然崩解特性，修护意在尽可能维护和修复文物。当保护与修护并用时，它们一方面为实体媒介与数字媒介预留了未来的发展空间；另一方面可以保持作品背后的原有含义不变。保护与修护技术在此虽放在了远期阶段，但它们在教育与文化机构里不属于全新课题。把这些互相交织的技术归在远期阶段正是因为认识到这项工作的艰巨性，涉及保护和修护一批数量正迅速增长的文化艺术作品——无论其格式是模拟的、数字原生的或是时基的。

除了保持媒介材料的物理状态之外，更需关注的问题是如何确保修护过程中媒介材料的意义完整不缺失。

在过去的几十年中，一些重要的机构已经开发出模型和标准，不断影响和改变着数字文档保护措施。1994 年，研究型图书馆组织与保护使用委员会组成数字信息归档专门小组，他们开发出了长期保存国家数字档案的系统，并首次将数字资源库作为解决方案的一部分。为了规范存储方法，他们设计了具有里程碑意义的开放档案信息系统，千禧年以来的联机计算机图书馆中心就是以这个信息系统为基础建立的。该框架系统涵盖了工作流程的各个技术层面，从数字对象的摄取到数据管理和访问，以及推荐相关的五种类型的元数据：参考信息、出处、背景、固有信息和描述信息。

在博物馆方面，数字文档的保护需要一批多面手型工作人员，他们必须掌握硬件技术，熟悉文件结构与格式、存储介质、电子处理器与芯片，同时兼备电气工程师、发明家和电脑科学家所需要的全部技能。除了专门展览计算机技术的博物馆之外，几乎没有博物馆具有解密文档内容，或是从几十年前的设备或存储介质中恢复资料的设备和专业知识。

保护工作一直是档案工作者、科学家以及图书馆的追求，而修护也许才是博物馆最需要做的事情。博物馆里大量的实物艺术品需要员工保持关注以保证其稳定性与可展示性。此外，纳入音频、视频、移动元素或需与互动的艺术装置也为修护工作增加了额外的复杂性，使实物和数字文档成为一体。除了保持媒体材料的物理状态之外，更需关注的问题是如何确保修护过程中媒体材料的意义完整不缺失。这就要求管理者向艺术家进行咨询，或者参考已逝艺术家的记录，以确保尽可能不失真地传达其最初的创作意图。

博物馆正在进入其数字藏品迅速超越其实体藏品的时代。

世界各地的博物馆里存有大量的电子媒体文档，从保护与修护角度来看它们都具有不同的挑战性，如陈旧的操作系统，硬件以及计算机程序。无论是光存储还是磁存储都会随着时间的推移而失效，时间长了，数据的可读性便逐渐消失。此外，上述这些挑战还没有包括一旦有合适的硬件来访问这些文档所涉及的文件格式和文件运行的问题。虽然我们不能完全预见未来的技术发展，但是越来越多的对于保护修护技术的探讨暗示着这些技术将会得到更好的认识，并在今后 4～5 年的时间里得到实际应用。

与博物馆教育及传播的关联性

博物馆正在进入其数字藏品迅速超越其实体藏品的时代。基于过时的技术基础创作的产品正面临逐渐偏移创作者本意的问题。虽然保护与修护对于保持博物馆藏品的完好状态和藏品的教育意义至关重要，但是充分了解纠正这些问题所需的具体策略和技术，以及培训一定数量的专业人员来具体实施这些策略和技术对博物馆来说具有持续的挑战性。

高校图书馆项目正在研究数字信息管理的新领域，同时为保护与修护最麻烦的时基资料与数字资料培养未来一代的博物馆人员。除了加强对档案理论和元数据标准的理解之外，学生们直接与当代艺术家合作，以确定为子孙后代保留作品完整性的最佳途径。

如何修护时基媒介信息是艺术博物馆的难题，因为这些资料通常由特殊机械部件组成或涉及的技术和文本格式相对陈旧。同时，这些资料还具有特定意图。例如，已故的影像艺术家和雕塑家白南准是以使用阴极射线管显示器和模拟电视信号制作艺术品而著称的。博物馆要持续维护与展示白的作品，就要求修复者与策展人员不断修订展示方式，这样做通常会使展示偏离作者的本意，直接影响参观者对作品的解读。

一方面博物馆迟迟没有出台针对数字文件与时基藏品的官方保护与修护政策和措施，另一方面档案馆和图书馆则在努力探索相关的技术解决方案。目前，国会图书馆正着手研究已经损坏的和正在恶化的历史录音文档。这个调查启发了最近的麦克阿瑟奖金获得者、音频保护主义者卡尔·哈勃，他以超高像素图像与特殊图像处理系统进行计算，制作模拟录音的声音。在2012年，其工作的重要文化意义得到彰显，因为他的技术使人们第一次听到了亚历山大·格雷厄姆·贝尔的声音。

《新媒体联盟地平线报告》对于保护修护技术的介绍具有重要意义。它表明，越来越多的博物馆意识到，如果不能更好地理解此问题的复杂性并采取相应行动的话，他们将在不久的将来会面临困难。到目前为止，基本没有可行的保护修护的实践模式；然而，将此问题归于长远目标，反映出博物馆对其越来越重视。

博物馆里保护修护应用技术采样如下：

> **展览和收藏** 作为建立更加全面的馆内修护项目的组成部分，达拉斯艺术博物馆开设了绘画修护工作室。绘画修护工作室以尖端技术为特色——包括数字X光系统，它不仅是一个研究和处理艺术作品的中心，还成为研究尖端修护技术的平台。参观者可以透过玻璃墙观察工作室的日常活动：go.nmc.org/pai。

> **市场营销和公共关系** 博物馆的博客增加了越来越多来自修护部门的内容，以此来让观众看到鲜为人知的幕后活动。大英博物馆博客上传了关于如何修护和展示"博街宝库"古罗马银币藏品的科学图像和 YouTube 视频：go.nmc.org/beau。

> **观众服务和无障碍服务** 在新当代艺术博物馆，名为 XFR STN 的媒介归档项目正在一个网络图书馆 archive.org 的开放展示上数字化并传播数字原生材料（这些材料的原有格式比较陈旧），为大量不同类型的访客，包括残障人士提供永久性访问权：go.nmc.org/newm。

保护和修护技术应用实例

下面的链接是对博物馆具有直接相关性的保护和修护实例：

澳大利亚最古老的文化进入数字时代

go.nmc.org/samuseum

随着南澳大利亚博物馆将其世界最大馆藏数字化，可以访问偏远的原住民社区远至 1830 年的家族历史、照片与工艺品。有些藏品会面向全球公开，而有些部分则因其文化敏感性而受到限制。

加拿大文化遗产信息网（CHIN）的数字资源长期保存工具包

go.nmc.org/chi

通过最近对其成员的调查，加拿大文化遗产信息网（CHIN）试图找出博物馆数字保护所面临的问题，并将发布数字资源长期保存工具包，工具包里面的文档将提供具体的步骤来确认散佚材料的潜在风险与影响，以及如何开展保护政策、计划与程序。

爱因斯坦大脑的高分辨率数字幻灯片

go.nmc.org/ape

APERIO ePathology 数字化了 550 张爱因斯坦大脑的幻灯片，这些幻灯片最初捐赠给了马里兰州国家健康和医学博物馆。这使全世界的研究人员、科学家和爱好者都能够看到病理学家托马斯·哈维博士编制的原始幻灯片，他在 1955 年曾对爱因斯坦的遗体进行了解剖。

古根海姆媒体修护实验室

go.nmc.org/gug

古根海姆博物馆推出了媒体修护实验室，以评估和监测图像与声音等时基媒介作品，包括视频、胶片、幻灯片、音频以及基于计算机技术的作品，因此具有时效性。

机器人辅助修复

go.nmc.org/rest

马德里雷纳·索菲亚博物馆机器人利用快速拍照对艺术品进行扫描，可以展示人眼所不能发现的裂痕、划痕和折痕、底层草图以及所有后续润色。机器人可以通过计算机远程控制全天候工作。

泰特时基媒介修护

go.nmc.org/tat

泰特时基媒介部门负责一系列修护活动，包括通过访问记录艺术家意图，为作品技术时效性做好计划与准备等。

收藏在斯坦福大学的沃尔特斯艺术博物馆手稿

go.nmc.org/walt

沃尔特斯艺术博物馆和斯坦福大学图书馆正在共同努力，以保护10万多件经过高分辨率处理的中世纪独有手稿的图片，他们的保存格式可以使学者们利用数字处理工具对手稿进行分析。

沃尔夫森博物馆实现数字化

go.nmc.org/wol

为了使在线目录搜索更具效率，佛罗里达州沃尔夫森博物馆为12万多件馆藏物品进行拍照，录入相关数据，包括作者姓名，起源年代地点以及创作的原始媒介。

延伸阅读

对于那些想要了解更多关于保护和修护技术的人，谨推荐下列文章与资源。

两全其美 (PDF)

go.nmc.org/smin

（韦恩·克劳夫，史密森学会，2013年）史密森学会的77页免费电子书介绍了对1400多万件藏品进行数字化的过程。作者阐述了尽管数字化藏品成本较高，博物馆还是选择应对挑战，跟上数字化时代的发展。

修护与数码影像——第1部分

go.nmc.org/osulab

（艾米·麦克罗伊,《大学图书馆》,2013年6月18日）俄亥俄州立大学的数字成像室的修护人员从业内视角展示了图书、手稿与文物等文化遗产的修护、固定以及最终数字化的过程。所有数字化作品都储存在俄亥俄州立大学知识数据库中，读者可以在线访问。

科学有助于艺术修护

go.nmc.org/ben

（格雷格·弗拉库斯,《美国之音》,2013年9月30日）通过与梵高其他作品的油漆取样对比，运用成像检验比较画布纹理，确定一幅在欧洲某阁楼发现的画作，为梵高作品。

向博物馆数字化保护政策迈进

go.nmc.org/digsig

（马德琳·谢尔顿,《信号》,2013年6月13日）某博物馆研究人员认为数字化保护领域对文化机构而言仍处于新生阶段，图书馆与档案馆位于数字化保护计划的前沿。她指出由 Rhizome 网站、古根海姆博物馆和泰特现代美术馆发起的时基媒介保护项目对其他博物馆保护策略的形成具有指导意义。

当艺术作品缺失时：修护人员面临数字考验

go.nmc.org/digart

（梅丽娜·瑞兹克,《纽约时报》,2013 年 6 月 9 日）当美国惠特尼艺术博物馆得到最早的网络作品之一《世界上第一个合作性句子》时,修护者面临着概念层面上的争论,即如何维护作品的完整性,因其使用的 20 世纪 90 年代的编码媒介已经被淘汰。伴随着新的数字作品不断问世,文化机构必须培养此领域的专家。

当家庭作业变为实际工作：数字管理专业的学生帮助保护媒体艺术

go.nmc.org/cur

（乔恩·伊波利托,《静水博客》,2013 年 8 月 18 日）缅因州大学的数字管理专业的学生正在学习如何运用诸如"可变媒介调查问卷"等免费网络工具记录艺术家创造性作品的现行媒介淘汰后如何对作品进行修护的观点。古根海姆、惠特尼等博物馆以及朗格卢瓦基金会和 Rhizome.org 等档案馆都在使用该工具。

一些高校图书馆项目正在引领数字保存的新领域,它们对于培养未来新一代博物馆工作人员去应对保护和修护最棘手的时基数字材料的问题是有帮助的。

新媒体联盟地平线项目简介

本报告是始于 2002 年 3 月的对新兴技术进行纵向研究项目的一部分。自那时候起，在"地平线项目"的旗号下，新媒体联盟及其研究合作伙伴与其咨询委员会持续开展了一系列的学术讨论和对话。目前，咨询委员会成员超过了 850 人，包括技术专家、大学技术人员、高等院校领导、博物馆专业人员、教师和其他学校专业人士以及来自全球顶尖企业的代表。10 多年来，对这些讨论和对话进行了深入挖掘，得以在每年一度的《新媒体联盟地平线报告》中发布新兴技术。

目前新媒体联盟地平线项目已经到了第十一个年头，它一直致力于为全球教育领域教学、学习和创造性探究的新兴技术描绘蓝图。

目前新媒体联盟地平线项目已经到了第十一个年头，它一直致力于拓展全球教育领域，为教学、学习和创造性探究的新兴技术描绘蓝图。2008 年，新媒体联盟在三个地平线项目主报告之外，增加了一项以地区性和基于行业的研究为主的报告——《新媒体联盟技术展望》。出版该报告主要有两个目的：一是从更微观的视角来理解技术是如何被采纳的；二是比较不同领域之间技术应用的差别。

迄今为止，新媒体联盟已经开展了澳大利亚、新西兰、英国、拉丁美洲、巴西、新加坡、挪威等国家和地区技术应用方面的研究并把这些研究向欧洲扩展。2012 年，《新媒体联盟技术展望》已经扩展到了行业分析领域，迄今为止已出版了包含 STEM（科学、技术、工程、数学）+ 教育、社区，职业技术学校和专科院校等各个领域的技术采纳方面的研究报告。

经过精心挑选，2013 年的咨询委员会包括 44 名成员，广泛代表了博物馆的各个领域；来自博物馆、教育和商业、产业领域的主流作家、思想家、技术专家和未来学家构成了委员会的完美阵容。在广泛回顾分析了各类研究、文章、学术成果、博客以及访谈资料的基础上，他们针对已有的技术应用展开讨论，并通过头脑风暴，寻找新的技术应用，最后根据他们与博物馆教育和传播可能发生的关联性，对候选的技术种类进行排序。这些工作完全是利用在线工具展开的，感兴趣的读者可以访问项目的维基网站，网址是 museum.wiki.nmc.org。

2013 年 8 月，编写组开始撰写《新媒体联盟地平线报告（2013 博物馆版）》，历经三个多月，2013 年 11 月份，报告最终发布。前面的章节已经详细阐述了排名最靠前的六项技术和应用，每个预期投入应用阶段包含两项技术。

本报告每一章节包括对技术的详细描述，典型示范项目链接以及与六项技术相关的大量附加资源。这些描述是新媒体联盟地平线项目的核心。

《新媒体联盟地平线报告（2013年博物馆版》将推动新媒体联盟地平线项目全年的工作。为了能够方便公众与新媒体联盟分享教育技术项目，便于将来在新媒体联盟的地平线报告、项目导航数据库或者项目周刊 Tech Weekly（NMC Horizon EdTech Weekly App）上发表自己的成果，您可以访问网址 go.nmc.org/projects. 如果您想进一步了解《新媒体联盟地平线系列报告》制作的方法和过程——其中的许多方法和过程仍在持续进行并拓展了报告中的工作——我们推荐您阅读本报告的最后一部分，该部分主要介绍了研究方法。

经过精心挑选，今年的咨询委员会包括 44 名成员，广泛代表了博物馆的各个领域；来自博物馆、教育和商业、产业领域的主流作家、思想家、技术专家和未来学家构成了委员会的完美阵容。

研究方法

本报告所用的研究方法与其他新媒体联盟地平线项目的研究方法同出一辙。新媒体联盟地平线报告系列的所有版本的诞生都经历了非常严谨的过程，既包含初级研究也有次级研究。针对每份报告，都要考察几十种技术，有意义的发展趋势以及面临的关键挑战来决定能否可以收录。每份报告的产生都建立在国际顶尖专家组成的咨询委员会的智慧之上。首先，委员会会在较宽广的范围内考虑一系列重要的新兴技术以及面临的挑战和发展趋势，然后，对其逐一进行越来越详细深入的考察，缩小之前所列的范围，直到最终选定将列入报告的技术、趋势和挑战。

> **针对每份报告，都要考察几十种新兴技术，有意义的发展趋势以及面临的关键挑战来决定能否可以收录。**

研究的过程采用在线方式开展，整个过程在新媒体联盟地平线项目的 wiki 上都有记录。设立该专题 wiki 的目的是为了能够完全透明地向大家展示项目工作的进展，完整记录研究过程中各个不同版本的情况。感兴趣的读者可以前往 museum.wiki.nmc.org 了解《新媒体联盟地平线报告（2013年博物馆版）》。

本报告采用了修订后的德尔菲法（专家调查法）来选定要包含的讨论主题，在新媒体联盟地平线系列报告多年的使用实践中，该方法已经被改进。首先是咨询委员会的组成，咨询委员会的成员有着多元化的背景、国籍和擅长的领域，但是每一位成员都为项目提供了特别相关的专业知识。在新媒体联盟地平线项目十多年的研究中，有超过 850 位获得国际认可的从业者与专家参加了项目咨询委员会，每年都有三分之一的咨询委员会成员是新会员，以保证每年的报告可以融入新的观点。欢迎读者推荐咨询委员会的专家，具体操作方法参见网址 go.nmc.org/horizonnominate。

确定了咨询委员会的成员后，他们首

先要对相关文献进行系统的检视，包括新兴技术方面的报刊文摘、报告、论文以及其他材料。在项目开始时，每位咨询委员会的成员都会领取到一套关于该项目的广泛背景材料，然后针对材料发表自己的意见，找出其中特别有价值的部分并增加新的资料。委员会讨论现有的新兴技术的应用，同时通过头脑风暴发现新的技术应用。判断某项技术是否被选入报告的核心指标为：它是否会对博物馆教育与传播有潜在关联性。我们采用RSS订阅了数百份精心挑选的相关出版物，以保证项目组的背景资料随着项目的进展能得到及时更新。这些材料是激发参与者在整个过程中思考的源泉。

在完成文献检视后，咨询委员会成员将开展核心工作，也就是研究新媒体联盟地平线项目的核心问题。通过这些问题，咨询委员会将广泛罗列令人关注的技术、其面临的挑战以及发展的趋势。这些问题有：

1. 在新媒体联盟地平线项目所列的关键技术中，哪些会在未来的五年内对博物馆教育和传播起到最重要的作用？

2. 在当前的列表中，还有哪些关键技术被漏列？请思考以下相关问题：

> 请列出在一些机构正在使用的现有技术中，哪些应该推广到所有的博物馆，用以支持和提升博物馆教育和传播？

> 哪些在消费者、娱乐或其他行业有着坚实用户基础的关键技术博物馆也应积极采纳？

> 你认为有哪些重要的新兴技术已发展到这样一种程度，以至于需要博物馆在未来4～5年内需要关注？

3. 在未来五年，你认为博物馆教育和传播面临的重大挑战有哪些？

4. 对于博物馆而言，哪些发展趋势会对它们以技术实现教育与传播的使命和目标产生重要影响？

咨询委员会最重要的任务之一就是尽可能系统而广泛地回答以上问题，以保证其充分考虑所有相关的主题。这项工作进展非常迅速，也就是用了几天的时间。接下来咨询委员会将进入达成共识的阶段，该阶段将采用迭代式的德尔菲法进行。

在该方法的第一阶段，每个咨询委员会成员都要使用多重投票系统进行投票。该系统允许成员们对他们的选择加上相应的权重，用这种方式对以上问题的回答进行系统排序并归纳到相应的预期投入应用阶段当中。每名成员还要对技术进入主流应用的时间进行判断。所谓主流应用，就本项目而言定义为在相应时间段内有20%的机构采用这项技术（该数据来源于乔弗雷·摩尔的研究，他界定了技术进入广泛应用所需的使用数量）。随后，这些排序数据都被收集在一起，于是大家的意见便可以相对集中了。

我们从最初为报告选择的一系列技术中选择了首轮排序靠前的 12 项技术（每个预期投入应用阶段有 4 项技术）做进一步研究讨论。一旦这 12 项技术的"候选列表"确定后，咨询委员会成员、新媒体联盟的员工和领域内的其他从业人员一起讨论该如何将这 12 项重要的技术应用于博物馆教育与传播。在这个阶段会花费大量的时间研究每一项技术在从业者们感兴趣的各个领域的真实应用和潜在应用。

当上述工作完成后，我们就会按照《新媒体联盟地平线报告》的格式将"候选列表"中的 12 项技术全部编写出来。这份"候选列表"既能够全面展现 12 项技术在报告中的全貌，又会被作为排序的依据。这次是逆排序，最后的六项技术和其应用将会在《新媒体联盟地平线报告》中详细阐述。

如果您想了解该项目更详细的研究方法或查看实际的研究工具、排序过程以及中期成果，请访问网址：museum.wiki.nmc.org。

新媒体联盟地平线项目
2013 年博物馆版咨询委员会名单

Larry Johnson
Co-Principal Investigator
New Media Consortium
United States

Koven Smith
Co-Principal Investigator
Denver Art Museum
United States

Holly Witchey
Co-Principal Investigator
Johns Hopkins University
United States

Samantha Adams Becker
Lead Writer/Researcher
New Media Consortium
United States

Alex Freeman
Editor
MIDEA
United States

Susana Smith Bautista
University of Southern California
United States

Allegra Burnette
Museum of Modern Art (MOMA)
United States

Suse Cairns
MuseumGeek Blog
Australia

Sheila Carey
Canadian Heritage Information Network
Canada

Erin Coburn
Consultant
United States

David Dean
Museum of Texas Tech University
United States

Guy Deschenes
PhD Candidate, Museology, UQAM
Canada

Ryan Donahue
The Metropolitan Museum of Art
United States

Jennifer Foley
Cleveland Museum of Art
United States

Vivian Kung Haga
Balboa Park Online Collaborative
United States

Susan Hazan
The Israel Museum, Jerusalem
Israel

Phyllis Hecht
JHU Museum Studies
United States

Jessica Heimberg
Dallas Museum of Art
United States

Nik Honeysett
J. Paul Getty Museum of Art
United States

Lynda Kelly
Australian National Maritime Museum
Australia

Eli Kuslansky
Unified Field
United States

Rob Lancefield
Davison Art Center, Wesleyan University
United States

Miriam Langer
New Mexico Highlands University
United States

Jack Ludden
J. Paul Getty Trust
United States

Elizabeth Merritt
AAM
United States

Jonathan Munar
Art 21
United States

Mike Murawski
Portland Art Museum
United States

Liz Neely
Art Institute of Chicago
United States

Lorna O'Brien
North Lands Creative Glass / Timespan Museum and Arts Centre
Scotland

Lori Byrd Phillips
The Children's Museum of Indianapolis
United States

Victoria Portway
Smithsonian National Air and Space Museum
United States

Mia Ridge
Museums Computer Group / Open University / Open Objects Blog
United Kingdom

Ed Rodley
Peabody Essex Museum
United States

Adrianne Russell
Marianna Kistler Beach Museum of Art
United States

Suzanne Sarraf
National Gallery of Art
United States

Scott Sayre
Sandbox Studios
United States

Marsha Semmel
Noyce Leadership Institute / Independent Consultant
United States

John Stack
Tate
United Kingdom

Len Steinbach
Steinbach and Associates
United States

Robert Trio
Hong Kong Maritime Museum
Hong Kong

Don Undeen
The Metropolitan Museum of Art
United States

John Weber
Institute of the Arts and Sciences, University of California, Santa Cruz
United States

Heather Marie Wells
Crystal Bridges Museum of American Art
United States

Bruce Wyman
Bruce Wyman & Associates
United States

NMC Horizon Report > 2013 Museum Edition

The NMC Horizon Report: 2013 Museum Edition is a publication of The New Media Consortium and the Marcus Institute for Digital Education in the Arts

The Edward and Betty Marcus Institute for Digital Education in the Arts (MIDEA) provides timely, succinct, and practical knowledge about emerging technologies that museums can use to advance their missions. Learn more at midea.nmc.org.

© 2013, The New Media Consortium.

ISBN 978-0-9897335-2-6

Permission is granted under a Creative Commons Attribution License to replicate, copy, distribute, transmit, or adapt this report freely provided that attribution is provided as illustrated in the citation below. To view a copy of this license, visit creativecommons.org/licenses/by/3.0/ or send a letter to Creative Commons, 559 Nathan Abbott Way, Stanford, California 94305, USA.

Citation
Johnson, L., Adams Becker, S., Freeman, A., (2013). The *NMC Horizon Report: 2013 Museum Edition*. Austin, Texas: The New Media Consortium.

Cover Photograph
Photo by Visit El Paso: "El Paso Exploreum Museum."
www.flickr.com/photos/visitelpaso/9472999585

Inside Front and Back Cover Photograph
Photo by Canadian Film Centre: "Technological Displacement." www.flickr.com/photos/cfccreates/6207812935

Design by emgusa.com

Executive Summary

The internationally recognized *NMC Horizon Report* series of global analyses and the regionally-focused *NMC Technology Outlook* series are part of the NMC Horizon Project, a research effort established in 2002 that identifies and describes emerging technologies likely to have a large impact over the five years following the publication of each edition in formal and informal education around the globe. This volume, the *NMC Horizon Report: 2013 Museum Edition*, examines emerging technologies for their potential impact on and use in education and interpretation within the museum environment. The hope is that the report is useful to museums worldwide, and the international composition of the advisory board reflects the care with which a global perspective was assembled. While there are many localized factors affecting the adoption and use of emerging technologies in museums, there are also issues that transcend regional boundaries, and this report was created with these challenges in mind. The *NMC Horizon Report: 2013 Museum Edition* is the fourth in an annual series of museum-focused reports co-produced by the NMC and the Marcus Institute for Digital Education in the Arts (MIDEA).

Each of the three global editions of the *NMC Horizon Report* — higher education, primary and secondary education (K-12), and museum education — highlights six emerging technologies or practices that are likely to enter mainstream use within their focus sectors over the next five years. Key trends and challenges that will affect current practice over the same period frame these discussions.

The six technologies featured in the *NMC Horizon Report: 2013 Museum Edition* are placed along three adoption horizons that indicate likely timeframes for their entrance into mainstream use for museum education and interpretation. The near-term horizon assumes the likelihood of entry into the mainstream for museums within the next 12 months; the mid-term horizon, within two to three years; and the far-term, within four to five years. It should be noted at the outset that the *NMC Horizon Report* is not a predictive tool. It is meant, rather, to highlight emerging technologies with considerable potential for our focus areas of education and interpretation. Each of the six is already the target of work at a number of innovative museums and organizations around the world, and the projects and exhibits we showcase here reveal the promise of a wider impact.

Near-term Horizon

On the near-term horizon—that is, within the next 12 months—are two rapidly unfolding topics: *BYOD* and *crowdsourcing*. Both encompass ways for visitors to engage with museums on a deeper level, whether personalizing their devices with museum content or sharing ideas and observations that could become part of an exhibit. BYOD has largely arisen from staff needs, as museum employees increasingly want to work with their own laptops, which already contain the productivity tools they prefer. Crowdsourcing is not a new concept, but when integrated with social media and crowdfunding websites it is allowing patrons to play a more active role in the development of exhibits, catalogs, and databases.

> **BYOD** or "Bring Your Own Device" is a practice that has emerged as a result of the increasing number of people who take their laptops and other devices with them everywhere they go for maximum productivity. The BYOD movement is an effort by institutions to move away from a top-down system of providing technology to facilitate productivity, and instead simply provide the networks and contextual frameworks to coordinate the use of personal computing devices. As more people

rely on smartphones to navigate in their daily lives, the potential for museums to engage and reach visitors via their devices is vast. Many museums offer mobile apps for wayfinding, sharing, and curating purposes, taking the pressure off of institutions to purchase devices in bulk to lend to patrons. The workflow within cultural institutions has been similarly disrupted by BYOD as museum personnel are conducting their day-to-day work with their own personal computers. In a time when most software is web-based and technology is ubiquitous, the trend toward BYOD is stronger than ever, and best practices for museums are emergent as pioneers set policies and precedence.

> **Crowdsourcing** refers to a set of methods that leverage the ideas and work of a community of individuals around a common goal. Wikipedia is perhaps the most recognizable example of crowdsourcing as it relies on the work of thousands of volunteers who all share the task of compiling and editing historical and contemporary research in an open platform. Many museums use crowdsourcing to promote community engagement through social media, prompting visitors to submit observations and media to add an interactive dimension to events and exhibits. One of the most promising aspects of crowdsourcing has been its ability to reach large numbers of individuals who each contribute a small amount of money to fund a small- or large-scale project. In 2012, money raised for art-related projects through the crowdfunding site Kickstarter surpassed that of the National Endowment for the Arts for the first time. Beyond fundraising, cultural institutions are also crowdsourcing metadata for artworks and artifacts that have yet to be described, including the addition of alt-text to serve the visually impaired.

Mid-term Horizon

In the second adoption horizon, two to three years out, two technologies are expected to pass the 20% adoption point that marks entry into mainstream practice in the Horizon Project framework: these are *electronic publishing* and *location-based services*. Electronic publishing is transforming content workflows at museums across the world, as there is more pressure to share catalogs, apps, and other publication formats that contain rich media and interactive features. Location-based services help visitors navigate the museum space, often based on personal preferences. This topic is poised for rapid growth with major companies, including Apple and Google, purchasing startups that specialize in locational intelligence and indoor GPS.

> **Electronic publishing** is creating a sea change in how people consume media, research, news, and narratives. Major media companies like *The New York Times* and *Newsweek* are setting the standard for what electronic publishing can accomplish. Rich in digital media assets such as video, images, and audio, these digital building blocks can be easily deployed in a variety of media formats aimed at discrete audiences — a notion that has huge implications for expanding the reach of a museum's content. Cultural institutions generally still have much to do to make the conversion to electronic publishing workflows, including adopting design processes that leverage digital media for multiple dissemination channels. The Getty's Online Scholarly Catalogue Initiative has brought online publishing to the forefront for museums by providing them with the tools and framework they need to modernize their media production. The next step is to generate sustainable systems for the management and re-purposing of digital assets, as well as designing content to fit various mobile platforms.

> **Location-based services** are already so integrated into people's daily lives that few think twice before allowing mobile apps on their devices to track their location. Enabled by WiFi access points, GPS, enhanced RFID tags, and crowdsourced positioning technologies like Waze, location-based services are now able to resolve location very precisely, even indoors, and deliver up-to-the-moment information that is related to that particular spot. The social media check-in app FourSquare, now several years old, has become one of the most successful examples of how this technology can be adopted seamlessly into an individual's life, rewarding users for tagging and sharing

their location. For museums, location-based apps and other technologies can knowingly guide visitors through a space, directing them to exhibits that match their preferences, or suggesting routes with accompanying digital displays and features to interact with. Museum professionals and programmers are discovering that location-based services in the museum space can streamline a visitor's cultural experience in memorable and meaningful ways.

Far-term Horizon

On the far-term horizon, set at four to five years away from entry into the mainstream of practice, are *natural user interfaces* and *preservation and conservation technologies*. Exhibits that make use of natural user interfaces that react to touch, movement, voice, and facial expression are going to be more intuitive for museum patrons, providing them ways to interact with artworks and installations. For years, museum professionals have been exploring ways to protect and repair both physical and digital objects that are in peril of becoming obsolete, due to rapidly changing technologies. Establishing workflows for developing and archiving metadata, in addition to documenting the artist's original intent, will be key for the advancement of preservation and conservation. These technologies are several years away from mainstream use, but already it is clear that their impact will be significant. The high level of interest and investment in both areas are indicators that they are worth following closely.

> **Natural user interfaces** (NUIs) are closing the gap between humans and computers as new platforms emerge that incorporate touch, voice, and other gestures. Smartphone and tablet users are most familiar with the ease of a natural user interface, but technologies beyond the touchscreen are rapidly advancing to make human-computer interaction even more intuitive. It is not uncommon for people to use virtual assistants on their smartphones to request and receive information, send texts and email, or use location data, rather than via touchscreen. These technologies are compelling museums to rethink the way visitors engage with art and objects, and there are a fair share of museums that have already incorporated tablets and multi-touch displays that reinvent exhibits and allow visitors to become a part of installations. Microsoft Kinect, a gesture-based technology that uses motion sensors, is being used more frequently, inviting visitors to interact with digital renditions of delicate objects. The latest development in NUIs is the integration of texture

Each of the three global editions of the *NMC Horizon Report* — higher education, primary and secondary education (K-12), and museum education — highlights six emerging technologies or practices that are likely to enter mainstream use within their focus sectors over the next five years.

into otherwise normal touchscreens that allows users to sense a wide range of tactile stimuli. Ultimately, natural user interfaces offer museums opportunities to leverage emerging technologies to more deeply engage visitors in the artworks and artifacts.

> **Preservation and conservation technologies** are often used interchangeably in conversation, but they are distinct in their purposes. While preservationists protect artifacts from obsolescence by safeguarding their intention and medium, conservators repair and restore objects that are subject to the trials of time. Digital archives were among the first technological solutions

implemented by preservationists, and have since generated a new standard of professionals that specialize in archival theory with technical expertise in developing tools to manage metadata. In addition to digitizing delicate artifacts, those charged with maintaining cultural heritage face a host of considerations when it comes to time-based media works that were originally executed using a technology that has become obsolete. The main challenge of a modern preservationist is to present content in workable ways that stay true to the artist's intent. As technologies to facilitate the preservation and conservation of digital and physical objects become more sophisticated, institutions such as the Library of Congress are setting the standard in the most innovative methods of upholding the integrity of cultural objects.

To create the report, an international body of experts in museums, education, technology, and other fields was convened as an advisory board. Over the course of August through September of 2013, the 2013 Horizon.Museum advisory board came to a consensus about the topics that appear here in the *NMC Horizon Report: 2013 Museum Edition*. The examples and readings under each topic area are meant to provide practical models as well as access to more detailed information.

Six technologies are described in detail in the main body of the report, where a discussion of what each technology is and why it is relevant to museum education and interpretation can also be found. Our research indicates that all six of these technologies have clear applications in museum learning and interpretation, and this report aims to document that in a simple and compelling fashion.

The group engaged in discussions around a set of research questions intended to surface significant trends and challenges and to identify a wide array of potential technologies for the report. This dialog was enriched by an extensive range of resources, current research, and practices that drew on the expertise of both the NMC community and the communities of the members of the advisory board. These interactions among the advisory board are the focus of the *NMC Horizon Report: 2013 Museum Edition* research, and this report details the areas in which these experts were in strong agreement. The precise research methodology employed is detailed in the closing section of this report.

The advisory board of 44 technology experts spanned six countries this year, and their names are listed at the end of this report. Despite their diversity of backgrounds and experience, they share a consensus view that each of the profiled topics is going to have a significant impact on museum education and interpretation around the globe over the next five years. The key trends driving interest in their adoption, and the challenges museums will need to address if they are to reach their potential, also represent their perspective, and are the focus of the next sections of the *NMC Horizon Report: 2013 Museum Edition*.

To facilitate comparison, the report's format is consistent from year to year and edition to edition, and opens with a discussion of the trends and challenges identified by the advisory board as most important for the next five years. The format of the main section of this edition closely reflects the focus of the NMC Horizon Project itself, centering on the applications of emerging technologies — in this case for museums. Each section is introduced with an overview that describes what the topic is, followed by a discussion of the particular relevance of the topic to museum education and interpretation. Several concrete examples of how the technology is being used are given.

Finally, each section closes with an annotated list of suggested readings and additional examples that expand on the discussion in the report. These resources, along with a wide collection of other helpful projects and readings, can all be found in the project's open content database that is accessible via the NMC Horizon EdTech Weekly App for iOS (go.nmc.org/ios) and Android (go.nmc.org/android) devices . All the background materials for the *NMC Horizon Report: 2013 Museum Edition*, including the research data, the preliminary selections, the topic preview, and this publication, can be downloaded for free on iTunes U (go.nmc.org/itunes-u).

Key Trends

The technologies featured in each edition of the *NMC Horizon Report* are embedded within a contemporary context that reflects the realities of the time, both in the sphere of museum education and in the world at large. To assure this context was well understood, the advisory board engaged in an extensive review of current articles, interviews, papers, and timely research to identify and rank trends that were currently affecting the practice of museum education and interpretation. Once detailed, the list of trends was then ranked according to how significant each was likely to be for museums in the next five years. The highest ranked trends had significant agreement among the advisory board members, who considered them to be key drivers of museum technology adoptions for the period 2013 through 2018. They are listed here in the order in which the advisory board ranked them.

1 Cross-institution collaboration is growing as an important way to share resources. Museums are increasingly aware of the ways in which content, including but not limited to unmediated collections data, may be seen and used in the broader networked environment. The days of large-scale, multi-year, foundation-funded collaborative projects are probably on the wane. Increasingly, multi-institutional collaboration will occur at the data level with institutions being collaborative partners only in a passive sense, and the real work of pulling multiple resources together being accomplished downstream, possibly by third-party organizations.

2 Collection-related rich media are becoming increasingly valuable assets in digital interpretation. Museums are beginning to see the value in developing formal strategies for capturing high-quality media documentation at every opportunity. Curators and content specialists are working more closely than ever with educators and technologists to embrace opportunities provided by using digital resources to enhance multimodal learning both online and in the galleries. Video, audio, and animations are no longer seen as afterthoughts in interpretation but increasingly as necessary components of an interpretive plan. This trend is beneficial to museum professionals and visitors alike as it encourages a deeper understanding of objects, ideas, and audiences.

3 Digitization and cataloguing projects continue to require a significant share of museum resources. Museums are distinguished by the content they keep and interpret. There is an increasing understanding among museum professionals that visitors expect to be able to readily access accurate and interesting information and high-quality media. This requires museums to plan strategically for the digitization and cataloging of collections. These projects frequently require sacrifices in terms of scarce resources (money, personnel, and time) in order to meet long-term goals.

4 Expectations for civic and social engagement are profoundly changing museums' scope, reach, and relationships. More and more, museums are integrating emerging technologies and approaches such as social media, open content, and crowdsourcing as a means of engaging their communities both internally and externally on a deeper level. Embracing these innovations means that museums are providing patrons with more immersive opportunities to become part of the content. Increasingly, people who are unable to make a physical trip to a museum are able to access its collections and respond and contribute meaningfully to conversations about what may be happening in the physical space, redefining what it means to be a museum patron.

5 **Increasingly, visitors and staff expect a seamless experience across devices.** Whether viewing objects in gallery spaces, ordering tickets, interacting with the online store, or simply browsing the museum's website, visitors expect museums to provide a wide range of digital resources and content, and want the experience of interacting with that content to be consistent across their devices. Virtual visitors in particular expect to

Museums are beginning to see the value in developing formal strategies for capturing high-quality media documentation at every opportunity.

be able to perform typical tasks online quickly and easily irrespective of the device they may have at hand. This is true even for visitors in the physical space, where it is common to see people interacting with their smartphones as they decide which part of the gallery to visit next.

6 **More and more, people expect to be able to work, learn, study, and connect with their social networks wherever and whenever they want.** We are not tied to desks anymore when we wish to use computers. Workers increasingly expect to be able to work from home or from the road, and most everyone expects to be able to get information, addresses, directions, reviews, and answers whenever they want. This is a key trend for both museum professionals and museum visitors. Mobile access to information is changing the way we plan everything from outings to errands. A corollary of this trend is the expectation that people will be available and online, anywhere and anytime.

7 **The need for data literacy is increasing in all museum-related fields.** Ninety percent of the world's data has been created in the last two years, and, through the exponential growth of hardware, software, and networking, every day we add 2.5 quintillion bytes. Important societal decisions in the near future will be informed by big data, and for individuals, as informed citizens, to fully engage in these conversations the ability to read and interpret large data sets will become increasingly necessary. Additionally, one in five Americans does not use the Internet because of a lack of knowledge, lack of affordable access to computers and the Internet, or because they do not understand its inherent value. These individuals are at risk of being left behind the digital divide, and libraries and museums have the opportunity to reach out to these communities to ensure people gain the digital literacy skills needed to succeed in the 21st century.

Significant Challenges

Any discussion of technology adoption must also consider important constraints and challenges, and the advisory board drew deeply from a careful analysis of current events, papers, articles, and similar sources, as well as from personal experience, in detailing a long list of challenges museums face in adopting any new technology. Several important challenges are detailed below, but it was clear that behind them all was a pervasive sense that constraints existing within museums themselves are likely the most important factors in any decision to adopt—or not to adopt—a given technology.

Even institutions that are eager to adopt new technologies may be critically constrained by the lack of necessary human resources and the financial wherewithal to realize their ideas. Still others are located within buildings that simply were not designed to provide the radio frequency transparency that wireless technologies require, and thus find themselves shut out of many potential technology options. While acknowledging that local barriers to technology adoptions are varied and meaningful, the advisory board focused its discussions on challenges that are common to museums and the museum community as a whole. The highest ranked challenges they identified are listed here, in the order in which the advisory board ranked them.

1 Greater understanding is needed of the relationships, differences, and synergies between technology intended to be used within the museum and public-facing technology such as websites, social media, and mobile apps. Too few in museum administration see the opportunities that virtual museum visitors might be bringing for fundraising, philanthropy, and specialized marketing. The dichotomy between the physical and virtual museum visitor is blurring rapidly, and both audiences have high expectations with regard to online access to services and information. Still, the notion that museums must provide comprehensive information and services online is a genuine challenge, especially for smaller museums. For larger institutions, however, providing such services has risen to an expectation from the visiting public.

2 Museums of all sizes are struggling to adapt to how technology is redefining staff roles and organizational structures. The pervasiveness of technology in almost all aspects of the museum has had a dramatic effect on the importance of digital departments; they now need to work both horizontally (coordinating and interacting with many other departments) and vertically (needing leadership and strategic oversight). Furthermore, as the digital realm increasingly touches all aspects of the museum from education and marketing to research and curating, these activities start to blur and merge into each other. Navigating this shift requires new skills both in the digital team and across the whole organization. At the Tate, for example, they are starting a comprehensive organizational change project centered on the museum's digital strategy.

3 A comprehensive digital strategy has become a critically important part of planning for long-term institutional sustainability. Such a strategy should include not only traditional elements of a technology plan (e.g., hardware, software, networks, etc.) but also e-forms of marketing, philanthropy, and revenue generation, as well as critical tasks like digitization, digital preservation, and long term technology infrastructure. This plan should "future-proof" the museum to every extent possible, by ensuring that they have accounted for all infrastructure needs. Additionally, it is clear that a museum cannot simply plan a web presence as it might a brochure or catalog — a museum's digital presence today includes not only a website, but also a social media presence, mobile tools and apps, interaction with online communities, electronic fundraising, online sales, and much more. All must be addressed, as will the skill sets that will be required.

4 In many cases, museums may not have the necessary technical infrastructure in place to realize their vision for digital learning. In the United States alone there are around 17,000 institutions that self-identify as museums; many of these institutions have few staff and fewer resources. While it is practically impossible not to recognize the value of digital learning in today's connected world, the reality for museums is that the vast majority of institutions do not have the necessary technical infrastructure to successfully pursue goals for

> A comprehensive and sustainable digital asset management strategy is more important than ever to address the need to create, manage, discover, and deliver digital material effectively and productively.

digital learning, and often have little time to dedicate to articulating, much less realizing their vision. Museums that do have resources may have to choose to reallocate funds from non-digital education efforts in order to implement the necessary technical infrastructure.

5 As our disabled population increases as a percentage of overall population, and as a percentage of our active, engaged, museum-attending population, accessibility cannot be an afterthought. With more than 50 million Americans with disabilities, museums need to continue to improve the accessibility of facilities, exhibitions, and programs for this important population. In order to reach this audience, museums are investing more thought into the way educational programs and didactic materials are presented. Technology can aid in increasing accessibility by breaking down barriers. Haptic technology, for example, enables blind and partially sighted individuals to touch virtual 3D objects. Additionally, museums can bridge this divide by creating special content for visitors with disabilities who are already bringing advanced technology along with them.

6 Museums are not doing a sufficient job of creating a sustainable environment to manage and deploy collection information and digital assets. The proliferation of destinations and platforms for collection information is becoming increasingly difficult to support and sustain. Collection data and digital assets including text, web, audio, video, and image files exist in multiple and largely unconnected locations, presenting often conflicting information. A comprehensive and sustainable digital asset management strategy is more important than ever to address the need to create, manage, discover, and deliver digital material effectively and productively.

These trends and challenges are a reflection of the impact of technology in almost every aspect of our lives, and across the museum sector. They are indicative of the changing nature of the way we communicate, access information, connect with peers and colleagues, learn, and even socialize.

Taken together in the context of the NMC Horizon Project research, they provided the advisory board a frame through which to consider the potential impacts of nearly 50 emerging technologies and related practices that were analyzed and discussed for potential inclusion in this edition of the *NMC Horizon Report*. Six of those were chosen as key; they are detailed in the main body of the report.

BYOD
Time-to-Adoption Horizon: One Year or Less

The term BYOD, which stands for "Bring Your Own Device," refers to the practice of people bringing their own laptops, tablets, smartphones, or other mobile devices with them to the learning environment. Intel coined the term in 2009, when the company observed that an increasing number of its employees were using their own devices and connecting them to the corporate network. Since then, this type of activity has become commonplace in workplaces all over the globe. The BYOD movement in museums is being driven by a major challenge that many institutions face — a lack of funds and infrastructure to support providing a device to every staff member or volunteer, much less patrons. BYOD leverages the devices that people already have. In early studies, the act of an individual using his or her own device has proven to increase productivity and engagement. With their ever-growing capabilities, tablets (which now include an expanding set of choices, such as the iPad, Galaxy, Nexus, and Surface) are well positioned for BYOD environments.

Overview

For museums and other education institutions, BYOD is less about the devices and more about the personalized content that users have loaded onto them. Rarely do two devices share exactly the same content or settings, and BYOD enables individuals to leverage the tools that make them most efficient and productive. Today, separating a user from their tools and apps has become like separating them from some of their most precious belongings. Devices have become the gateways to personal working and learning environments that are rich with interactive features that facilitate the exploration of new subjects and connect people with each other wherever they go. In this sense, the work environment has transcended the concept of staff being tethered to a desk and confined to a physical space, opening them up to the limitless productivity possibilities that exist across the Internet and its vast array of downloadable apps.

This notion of BYOD originated with Intel when they launched a personal device program in 2010. Today, the initiative supports around 25,000 of their personnel's smartphones, which they report has added nearly an hour more of productivity for employees each day, in addition to boosting morale. Intel has led the move away from institutional decisions and ownership of technology towards individual choice. When applied to museum staff, BYOD policies foster greater freedom and flexibility in the work environment and often eliminate unsecured devices. An increasing number of personnel are opting to bring their own laptops to the museum, which enables them to more seamlessly complete tasks, even when they are outside of the building.

The convenience of BYOD for museum staff has also prompted a shift in how the visitor experience is conceived. While traditionally museums have provided patrons with devices to accompany audio tours, they are now encouraging the use of personal smartphones and tablets in the space. This shift is largely due to the proliferation of mobile apps — perhaps the fastest growing dimension of the mobile space. Apps are key drivers of device personalization as users can choose from an array of educational and productivity resources that speak most to their work and interests.

A recent report from Gartner predicted that

102 billion apps would be downloaded in 2013 — or nearly 15 apps per each human being on Earth. As of October 2013, the regularly updated online app counter 148Apps reveals that there are more than 86,000 active educational apps in the iTunes store alone, making education the second most popular category, behind games. Most museums, especially the large ones, are taking advantage of this traction and have created their own apps to enhance the BYOD visitor experience with audio tours and supplemental materials, while also extending the learning activities and interactions outside of the physical space.

Relevance for Museum Education and Interpretation

The proliferation of mobile devices, coupled with the growing number of mobile apps, has had a tremendous effect on museums' mobile strategies, whether through the creation of mobile websites and apps, providing free WiFi access, or supplementing guided tours on museum owned devices with content for visitors' devices. This movement is notable because it shifts museum resources from the maintaining and supplying of technology to the content and delivery of high quality multimedia experiences. While not entirely supplanting the traditional museum-provided mobile device, this is an area with a great deal of activity within museums.

While museum visitors expect to seamlessly connect to the Internet whenever and wherever they want, it has been museum staff who have been the primary motivators for museums to provide free WiFi access — the key to making BYOD work. Museums are increasingly working with contract and transient staff who need to provide their own devices to conduct their work, and in the case where museums do offer devices, often the quality of the device an employee owns is superior to what otherwise might be available. There is also a desire for many staff members to work in the gallery space, making an openly accessible WiFi signal of critical importance. Visitors can also easily connect to the web to access their social networks, conduct research outside of the museum, and use mobile apps specifically designed by the museum to enhance their experience on-site.

More museums are seeing the value of enabling visitors to own and customize museum content on their devices, as it is an important step for connecting education and interpretation inside and outside the museum. The Museo del Prado's Official Guide exemplifies the current wave of mobile apps to personalize a visitor's learning experience before, during, and after a visit. The mobile app offers learners with high quality images of artworks, customizable thematic tours, searchable indexes, and direct access to the Museo del Prado's Facebook and Twitter accounts.

The ubiquity of smartphones with professional cameras and social apps has affected how museums are accommodating visitors who use these devices in the museum space. Today, it is not uncommon for museums to feature screens in the gallery spaces that leverage social media feeds to encourage dialog among visitors. The Museum of Contemporary Art in Australia has a formal program called MCA Now that shares the story of the museum through the eyes of visitors and staff, with a stream of Instagram and Twitter feeds displayed on monitors on each floor. The photographic impulse is also being recognized by museums as several large institutions, including the Metropolitan Museum of Art, Indianapolis Museum of Art, and Getty Museum have relaxed their policies to allow photography in some or all of their exhibition spaces — a direct response to the growing BYOD movement.

Though an increasing number of museums have revised their policies to embrace BYOD, it is not yet pervasive. Many museums are locked into long-term contracts with mobile guide vendors or have limitations — because of security, financial, or infrastructure issues — to provide free WiFi for visitors. Some museums still store and supply devices because it is less expensive than building and supporting a robust native app across a number of platforms.

Creating effective device-agnostic digital interpretives is a challenge that museums are currently in the midst of solving. Many museums are experimenting with revamping their websites to feature responsive design or building mobile websites to circumvent platform accessibility issues. Ultimately, as museums increasingly cater to BYOD, providing free WiFi will need to be considered an essential step.

A sampling of BYOD functions in museums includes the following:

> **Exhibitions and Collections.** "ArtLens" by the Cleveland Museum of Art is an iPad app that allows visitors to further explore collections in the museum or from home. Included in the app is indoor wayfinding technology that guides patrons to artworks that have interpretive content such as video and film along with a scanning feature that can recognize an image and offer content for it: **go.nmc.org/artl.**

> **Marketing and Communications.** Marketing departments are leveraging BYOD at special events by including backdrops and photobooths that encourage visitors to share their museum experience via social media. Mexic-Arte Museum often creates special areas in their exhibition spaces where patrons can take photographs of themselves re-enacting parts of artworks. **go.nmc.org/mexic.**

> **Visitor Services and Accessibility.** Museums can make their collections more accessible to deaf patrons with specialized apps for mobile devices. "SzépMűSL," an Android and iOS app that was recently created by Budapest's Museum of Fine Arts, features sign-language videos in several international sign languages for around 150 paintings from the museum's collections: **go.nmc.org/szep.**

BYOD in Practice

The following links provide examples of BYOD use in museum or other settings:

Bring Your Smartphone
go.nmc.org/dmaa
The Dallas Museum of Art website tells patrons to bring their smartphones in order to access content that has been specially developed for selected works in their collection. The institution also has a free WiFi network throughout, and encourages visitors to bring their laptops and other mobile devices to take advantage of the Internet café.

BYOD at Fashion Institute of Technology (PDF)
go.nmc.org/fitnewyork
The Fashion Institute of Technology (FIT) in New York has implemented a robust, secure wireless network that enables BYOD among 10,000+ students, faculty, and staff, and over 100,000 museum visitors annually. The aim was to eliminate the need for wired computer labs while maintaining quality of bandwidth in order to create more productive, flexible workspaces.

BYOD Keeps Hospital Group on Competitive Edge
go.nmc.org/nchhealth
NCH Health Systems, a hospital group in Florida, has implemented a two-part BYOD strategy for its two properties in an effort to promote an efficient, paperless work environment. Administrators are allowing employees to use their own devices for optimal convenience as well as publicizing the BYOD policy to gain a competitive edge when recruiting physicians.

BYOD Saves VMware $2 Million
go.nmc.org/vmware
Software company VMware, Inc. was a pioneer in BYOD, embracing the change in the fourth quarter of 2011. Since then, the company has managed to save $2 million on mobile phones alone due to their effective system for employee IT costs reimbursement. The savings were allocated toward improving infrastructure and R&D projects.

Capture the Museum
go.nmc.org/scot
A program at the National Museum of Scotland asks patrons to download the "Capture the

Museum" app to their phones to sign up for a physical team game in which players explore galleries to claim territories. The app was developed to enhance visitor engagement and to engage the newest generation of museum patrons.

MCA Insight
go.nmc.org/mca
The Museum of Contemporary Art Australia developed an app to provide an interactive accompaniment to the museum's collections, encouraging patrons to explore the stories behind installations and artworks through video and image. The app also includes a location awareness system that helps users find their way through the space with a responsive map.

QuizTrail
go.nmc.org/mid
Tate Britain's "QuizTrail" app guides visitors through the London gallery on themed trails ranging from "Animals" to "Myths and Legends," and they can earn prizes and discounts based on the number of questions they answer correctly for each tour. The app was designed to engage both children and adults in an immersive challenge that educates participants about British art.

For Further Reading

The following articles and resources are recommended for those who wish to learn more about BYOD:

4 Big BYOD Trends for 2013
go.nmc.org/byodinfo
(Michael Endler, *Information Week*, 21 February 2013.) Based on Gartner's evaluation of the uptake and implications of BYOD in enterprise, this author has highlighted four major trends that should concern every IT leader across sectors, including security and the use of BYOD as a recruitment tool.

BYOD: Six Tips for a Successful Implementation
go.nmc.org/success
(Sam Ganga, *Data Center Journal*, 7 October 2013.) There are many factors organizations must consider when developing a successful BYOD policy including security and technical concerns as well as creating a governance model to address new issues as they arise. This article provides a list of questions and points to cover in creating and implementing a BYOD policy.

Dear Museums: The Time is Right to Embrace Mobile
go.nmc.org/vis
(Matthew Petrie, *The Guardian*, 31 May 2013.) A recent study at the New York MoMA found that 74% of visitors brought a mobile device with them. The Victoria and Albert Museum in London commissioned a study that revealed that visitors would rather use their personal devices than a museum-provided device. Reasons included ease and familiarity, hygiene, and the convenience of already possessing an interpretation tool.

Education Efforts Key to Successful BYOD Programs
go.nmc.org/fierce
(David Weldon, Fierce Enterprise Communications, 10 October 2013.) Many organizations are either adopting formal BYOD policies or allowing informal BYOD use, but moving data across a variety of devices and networks means increased risk of leaks or attacks. Therefore, it is vital that each employee understand exactly how BYOD will work and how their behavior could lead to potential risks.

A Self Guided Tour App How-To
go.nmc.org/selfg
(*The Official Whitepoint Blog*, 17 August 2013.) This Whitepoint framework aims to help museums, galleries, and public spaces build and implement their own self-guided tour apps without costly development expenses. Visitors who bring their smartphones or tablets to the space can use the app to navigate through exhibits and collections.

Unavoidable: 62 Percent of Companies to Allow BYOD by Year's End
go.nmc.org/byodreport
(Teena Hammond, *ZDNet*, 4 February 2013.)

According to a global survey of over 1,000 ZDNet and TechRepublic members, more than 44% of organizations already allow BYOD and another 18% plan to implement BYOD by the end of 2013. The full report discloses the percentage of employees who participate in the program, the type of personal devices used most often for work, details regarding approaches to security, and the costs of the hardware and service plan.

What do Visitors Say about Using Mobile Devices in Museums?
go.nmc.org/vaml
(Andrew Lewis, Victoria and Albert Museum, 13 March 2013.) A series of surveys were conducted among a number of London museums to learn more about how patrons use their mobile devices and what they want in regards to content and services from museums. Findings from the Victoria and Albert Museum in particular describe a smartphone-toting museum visitor who is enthusiastic about free WiFi and desires content that is tailored to their interests and designed from a user needs perspective.

What is BYOD and Why is it Important?
go.nmc.org/byodtech
(Dean Evans, *Tech Radar*, 23 August 2013.) The consumerization of IT is forcing corporations and companies both large and small to develop strategies that maximize efficiency and reduce security risks. The key points of effective BYOD policy and implementation are outlined in this article for those that want to undertake the novel approach to IT management.

Crowdsourcing
Time-to-Adoption Horizon: One Year or Less

Crowdsourcing refers to a set of methods that can be used to motivate a community to contribute ideas, information, or content that would otherwise remain undiscovered. Its rapidly growing appeal stems from its effectiveness in filling gaps that cannot be bridged by other means. One of the most well-known examples of this is Wikipedia, where volunteers provide information and definitions for subject matter of their expertise. Crowdsourcing capitalizes on the power of explicit collective intelligence, where knowledge is constantly refined through the contributions of thousands of authors. For museum scholars, crowdsourcing is often a way for researchers to draw on public knowledge to provide missing historical or other specific details related to communities or families, complete large-scale tasks, or solve inherently complex issues. For many tasks, institutions are finding that amateur scholars or even people whose lives simply were contemporary to the event, object, images, or other research focus being documented are remarkably effective in providing deep-level detail around a topic or in documenting a large body of materials. Related to crowdsourcing in many ways is crowdfunding, an effort to raise money through a network of people — usually through resources on the Internet. Many organizations, especially start-ups, turn to online tools such as Kickstarter to finance new projects and products. Crowdfunding has been known to support many different activities, from helping communities recover from disasters to free software development.

Overview

Crowdsourcing is compelling to museums and individuals alike; people can engage around ideas and content with others to produce work that none of them alone would have been able to accomplish. Social media communities on platforms such as Facebook, Twitter, and many others have made it even easier for museums to share resources and garner input from large groups of people. However, the notion of crowdsourcing is not new as organizations have long requested input from members, fans, and other key groups. Perhaps the oldest known instance of crowdsourcing in action— without the support of the web — is when the Oxford English Dictionary opened a call for contributions of quotations and example usages of the words. Over 70 years, they received more than six millions submissions.

The millennium also yielded many scientific companies whose very livelihood depends on the results of crowdsourcing. Ancestry.com, 23andme, and others have leveraged the upswing of personal DNA testing to build vast databases of genetic information that help participants gain an understanding of their family histories. Large-scale citizen science projects, such as the Cornell Lab of Ornithology and Journey North, rely on bird and wildlife observations submitted by amateur scientists across the United States to inform their daily research and track migration patterns. Museums have begun conducting similar crowdsourced research for cultural sites and objects for which they are hoping to gather information from knowledgeable individuals.

Not only does crowdsourcing help museums gather explicit information about specific subjects or artifacts, but it also generates a deeper connection between the patron and the institution, building trust and allegiance in innovative ways. German philosopher Walter Benjamin was famous for surmising that true art is a conception between the artist and the audience, and crowdsourcing exemplifies this notion by turning the audience into active participants, as their contributions ultimately become part of the final piece.

Crowdfunding is one of the fastest growing areas of crowdsourcing, particularly due to the advent of Kickstarter, Crowdfunder, Indiegogo, and similar websites, where anyone with Internet access can be a philanthropist and support exciting new ideas and projects. Museums, artists, and all kinds of users pay a fee to campaign for financial support through these platforms. If they gain enough pledges to meet their fundraising target, the projects are funded, and the people who contributed become a part of the success story. In many cases, these people also get something in return for their support, whether it is the final product that is being funded or other benefits. There are even hierarchies where the more a person invests, the bigger the return for them when the project is funded.

Because they foster communities by nature, museums are well poised to leverage every dimension of crowdsourcing to invite patrons to become part of the experiences they offer. Many have already deployed successful small- and large-scale crowdsourcing programs, and the practice is sure to grow.

Relevance for Museum Education and Interpretation

For the first time in 2012, money raised for art-related projects through the crowdfunding site Kickstarter surpassed that of the National Endowment for the Arts. This signals a major shift in the landscape of fundraising, demonstrating the power of crowds to fundamentally change how people and museums interact with each other. People's opinions and actions are increasingly leveraged by museums, whether it is to inform the content of an exhibition or to help scholars collect data.

In a challenging economic climate, funding museum exhibitions has become more difficult and museums are finding other methods to supplement exhibition budgets. The concept of crowdfunding is not new; small groups of wealthy patrons who see the benefit in furthering a museum's mission often come together to financially support exhibitions. What is new is the method in which this type of fundraising is occurring, and the type of individual who contributes. An online Kickstarter campaign for a yoga exhibition at the Smithsonian's Freer and Sackler Galleries recently generated $170,000 from 600 individuals united by their common interest in a popular topic. Kickstarter anticipates this type of fundraising to grow as they have created a new museum category on their website.

Similar to how museums are asking individuals to invest with dollars, they are also looking to crowds to help inform their exhibitions, whether they are showcasing user-generated content or engaging with audiences in voting for their favorite artworks and artists. The Brooklyn Museum of Art is well known for the latter strategy; they invite their local museum community to visit Brooklyn area artist studios and vote for the artists they would like to see featured in group exhibitions.

Citizen science has converged with crowdsourcing in an interesting way to aid in the research of science museums that double as research centers. For example, Calbug is an effort to crowdsource and digitize information on more than one million insects and spiders contained in nine California natural history museums. Participants earn badges as they help transcribe data so that the information will be accessible to help inform researchers about changes in biodiversity.

The Cooper-Hewitt Museum is using crowdsourcing to generate descriptions for their vast collection of objects that have little to no metadata attached to them. Their new collection website offers the opportunity to provide information about an object through a built-in tagging feature. For example, at the bottom of an object's webpage, there is a note to tag personal photos from Flickr and Instagram or 3D models from SketchUp and Thingiverse to connect their collection to users' content.

Crowdsourcing tangibly reveals the power of collaboration and dialog as visitors increasingly expect to engage with museums in a more personal way. While crowdsourcing is becoming widely used, museums still need to overcome challenges in embracing user-generated content and feedback. A genuine crowdsourcing project requires museums to relax their authority over the content and welcome ideas that deviate from what was expected in order to foster the type of synergy that frequently leads to innovation.

A sampling of crowdsourcing applications in museums includes the following:

> **Exhibitions and Collections.** Map the Museum is an open data project where people go online to virtually place objects from the collections of the Brighton & Hove's Royal Pavilion and Museums on a local map, demonstrating the relationship between the city and the museum, while also creating new data that can become a part of each object's permanent catalog record: go.nmc.org/mapm

> **Marketing and Communications.** Matthew Inman, famously known as the Oatmeal, raised more than $520,000 over his $850,000 goal to build a Tesla Museum by harnessing the power of social media to share his Indiegogo crowdfunding campaign. The link to his campaign received 12,600 Twitter shares, 47,000 Facebook likes, and 9,700 Google +1's: go.nmc.org/tesla.

> **Visitor Services and Accessibility.** The Museum Victoria in Australia uses an open source, web-based program called Describe Me that crowdsources alt-text in an effort to make the collections online more accessible for people with visual impairments. Volunteers are presented with an image and then write a short description of what they see: go.nmc.org/desau.

Crowdsourcing in Practice

The following links provide examples of crowdsourcing in use in museum settings:

Agricultural Innovation and Heritage Archive
go.nmc.org/ament
The Smithsonian's National Museum of American History is asking visitors to contribute their personal narratives about technologies that have changed the history of farming and ranching in the United States, and to relate how these changes have impacted their communities. The goal is to compile a crowdsourced digital archive that will tell the narrative of American agriculture for the museum's American Enterprise exhibition.

ArtPrize
go.nmc.org/artpz
ArtPrize is an annual open art competition that takes place over 19 days in downtown Grand Rapids, Michigan, where anyone over the age of 18 can submit their work to be judged by the public, with an opportunity to win the first place award of $200,000. The contest is independently organized by a community of artists and sponsors.

Historypin
go.nmc.org/histp
Historypin is a collaboration between non-profit We Are What We Do and Google that asks people to add their media—photos, letters, and memories—to a public archive where artifacts are pinned to a location and searchable on Google Maps. The website also features collections that allow users to explore specific time periods and places through photos.

Marina Abramovic Institute: The Founders
go.nmc.org/abram
In July 2013, the Marina Abramovic Institute kicked off a campaign to crowdfund the $600,000 needed to construct a building to house what renowned performance artist Abramovic calls "long durational work," or the joining of art, science, technology, and spirituality. The campaign reached its goal, and those who contributed more than $1 will receive an embrace from Abramovic in return.

Puffing Gun
go.nmc.org/boom
The Museum of Food and Drink reached its goal of raising $80,000 through Kickstarter in order to fund the development of a puffing gun that turns grains into breakfast cereal, which was on display in Manhattan on three consecutive Saturdays. It was the first exhibition by founder Dave Arnold, a chef, radio host, and restaurateur.

Space Shuttle Enterprise: A Pioneer
go.nmc.org/intrepid
New York's Intrepid Sea, Air, and Space Museum created a crowdsourced exhibit for the space shuttle, Enterprise. The museum has asked the public to upload photographs of their space shuttle moments to the museum's website or post them to Instagram and Twitter with their own captions so that the museum can create a physical as well as online exhibition with the content.

Ten Most Wanted
go.nmc.org/tenmo
Developed for the Museum of Design in Plastics in the UK, Ten Most Wanted is a game-based approach to crowdsourcing the verification of undocumented facts about collection objects, requiring sustained engagement and collaboration among contributors. This model can be applied to other contexts, such as identifying people and places in paintings or photographs.

For Further Reading
The following articles and resources are recommended for those who wish to learn more about crowdsourcing:

Crowdsourcing Museums: Can Big Donors, Curatorial Decisions, and Individual Artists Be Replaced?
go.nmc.org/don
(Paula Newton, *Glasstire*, 31 May 2013.) This article provides examples of how museums are turning to crowdfunding, crowdvoting, and crowdsourcing to help them garner wider support in their efforts. The author suggests that before embarking on a crowdsourcing activity that museums should consider the repercussions of not meeting a funding goal or how general public opinion can affect the outcomes of art in a restrictive manner.

Digital Humanities and Crowdsourcing: An Exploration
go.nmc.org/anex
(Laura Carletti, Gabriella Giannachi, Dominic Price, Derek McAuley, *Museums and the Web*, 2013.) As cultural institutions are progressively exploring crowdsourcing, the authors of this paper drew from a web survey on 36 different crowdsourcing projects promoted by galleries, libraries, archives, museums, and education institutions to shed light on the variety of practices to support the development of crowdsourcing initiatives.

Oh Snap! Experimenting with Open Authority in the Gallery
go.nmc.org/ohsnap
(Nina Simon, *Museum 2.0*, 13 March 2013.) Carnegie Museum of Art's experimental photography project, "Oh Snap! Your Take on Our Photographs," allows in-person and virtual visitors to share their work in their own galleries. This post describes the benefits of this project and how the museum is engaged in an ongoing dialog with participants because of it.

On the Trickiness of Crowdsourcing Competitions: Some Lessons from Sydney Design
go.nmc.org/tricky
(Mia Ridge, *Open Objects*, 27 May 2013.) This article describes lessons learned from a competition held during the Sydney Design festival. The organization's crowdsourcing effort was perceived by some as an unethical way to get spec work from designers.

What is Crowdsourcing? And How does it Apply to Outreach?
go.nmc.org/out
(*idea*, 19 February 2013.) This overview of crowdsourcing breaks down the topic into multiple facets to explain exactly how it can benefit organizational outreach. From cloud labor to collective knowledge, there are many methods of harnessing support from the community.

Yes, Kickstarter Raises More Money for Artists Than the NEA. Here's Why That's Not Really Surprising
go.nmc.org/rai
(Katherine Boyle, *The Washington Post*, 7 July 2013.) Kickstarter has funded more than $600 million in arts projects by providing a platform that simplifies the long-held tradition of individual private donors giving to the arts. Individual donors giving money to the arts is nothing new — only the method of donating.

Electronic Publishing
Time-to-Adoption Horizon: Two to Three Years

Already firmly established in the consumer sector, electronic publishing is redefining the boundaries between print and digital, still image and video, passive and interactive. Modern digital workflows support almost any form in which content might appear, from traditional print to digital, web, video, and even interactive content. Building in the full spectrum of potential publishing avenues — print, web, video, mobiles and tablets, and interactives — from the beginning is not only a way to streamline production overall, but also to increase the reach of the materials produced by leveraging the content over a wide range of media. If the first revolution in electronic publishing was making publishing platforms accessible to anyone, the next phase is the linking of these platforms together to produce new combinations and new types of content. New concepts like the Online Scholarly Catalogue Initiative (OSCI) and Responsive Design will allow that content to be easily archived as well as ported to any device.

Overview

Electronic publishing allows museums to design and produce a piece irrespective of the format in which it may ultimately appear, and thus fosters the flexibility to easily port content into many different formats, providing patrons with a variety of reading options. With each format comes a unique experience that is constantly progressing to include more enhanced features at every turn. Now that electronic publications have become commonplace, all major magazines and periodicals have at least one electronic variant, if not many. Electronic publishing reflects the convergence of several different forms of digital media into a single stream of production — a notion that is now being widely experimented with across the museum sector.

Electronic publishing has developed considerably over the past two years since the topic was featured in the *NMC Horizon Report: 2011 Museum Edition*. In 2012, Pew published a study revealing that half of Americans access their news online, with that number climbing to 60% for

> **Responsive Design is an approach that ensures an optimal viewing experience on any device of an individual's choosing, whether via desktop, laptop, smartphone, or tablet.**

people under the age of 25. *The New York Times* website garners over 30 million unique visitors per month, while its print circulation has decreased to one million copies daily. Furthermore, major publications such as Encyclopedia Britannica and *Newsweek* have discontinued their print runs altogether in favor of a digital-only presence. Over 30 years ago, media mogul Rupert Murdoch predicted the death of print publishing, and his premonition is materializing into a reality with each passing year.

In the midst of this rapid growth, the industry has faced the inherent challenge of changing its strategies and workflows while the technology itself is still evolving. Publishing houses are leading the way. Since 2009, these companies have been deploying ever more streamlined processes for generating, producing, and marketing content. Before electronic publishing, there were not as many moving pieces, and the pieces themselves were more easily understood; publishing meant print, words, and perhaps pictures. Video and multimedia were distinct forms, but now such distinctions are hard to make — and, increasingly, the ultimate published piece includes all of that, as is the case with major newspapers, magazines, and websites.

Today, many museum content and marketing teams see themselves as media companies, producing content for whatever delivery formats will achieve the greatest reach. With the advent of emerging new formats, publishers are able to create different versions of a piece — i.e. an extended version with author interviews or with a "foldout" of glossy images — and tailor them to distinct audiences. Content is captured just once for a variety of potential applications. Additionally, mobile apps have become publications in their own respect, and museums are using them to publish photos and videos from collections and interviews with artists — with interactive features for people to connect with the material on a deeper level.

A new dimension of electronic publishing this year is its connection to new methods and approaches in design. Responsive Design, for example, is an approach that ensures an optimal viewing experience on any device of an individual's choosing, whether via desktop, laptop, smartphone, or tablet. In this approach, navigation adapts instantly to display size and aspect; content automatically resizes or even replaces itself, fluidly adapting what is on the screen to the current browser and screen dimensions.

Relevance for Museum Education and Interpretation

Recent developments, particularly the implementation phase of the Online Scholarly Catalogue Initiative (OSCI), have sparked the rise of more openly accessible content and the increased adoption of electronic publishing strategies by museums and their staffs. While there are many examples of electronic publications in the form of catalogs and mobile apps in larger museums, the development of viable business models is stalling widespread adoption.

When the Getty's Online Scholarly Catalogue Initiative began in 2008 to increase access to collections through the dissemination of scholarly research on the web, museums were just beginning to understand the potential of this new medium. Five years later, the nine museums involved in the project are now actively experimenting with different forms of web-based publishing and sharing their findings with the larger museum community. The new resources and workflows, combined with a formal platform in the OSCI toolkit, have heralded a new way of thinking about catalog production, content management, and digital strategy in museums. As the Art Institute of Chicago has experienced, scholars who may have been reluctant to create electronic publications before the initiative are now embracing the OSCI toolkit as a valuable research tool.

Historically, creating museum publications was an expensive undertaking due primarily to printing and copyright costs, but with the move to digital, image permissions have become more relaxed at institutions including the National Gallery of Art, British Museum, and the Rijksmuseum. Access to once hidden parts of a collection have increased and greatly benefited research.

Traditional publishing was also a time-consuming and compartmentalized process, where activities were primarily "siloed" within individual departments. With the rethinking of workflow, multiple departments are beginning to work together so that the development of web, mobile, print, and in-gallery experiences progress in parallel. A dramatic shift is now taking place as people are becoming more comfortable with the free online publishing world of Instagram and tumblr, and attitudes are changing as museum staff and boards of trustees become more inclusive of technology adoption in museums.

With the increased functionality inherent in electronic publications, individuals with disabilities can garner a greater appreciation of artifacts than ever before. The Umlauf Sculpture Garden and Museum has provided touch tours for students from the Texas School for the Blind since 1991, and recently was able to augment their touch tours with large-print materials on iPads. Using iBooks Author, the museum released an iBook that highlights seven sculptures in the collection by creating verbal descriptions for selected artwork and wayfinding information for navigating the Garden for blind and low-vision visitors. Additionally, because this form of publication is accessed on a tablet, visitors with moderate central vision are able to read with greater ease and speed because of the ability to adjust the brightness of the written material.

In addition to electronic publishing's embrace of the growing number of digital formats and media, the process makes it very easy to produce variations of a story whether scholarly in nature or for wider appreciation. The evolution of this topic involves thinking about electronic publishing not as a set of products but as a means of delivering resources in new and different ways. Because of the flexibility electronic publishing provides, a growing number of museums are adopting models where they create once and publish everywhere.

A sampling of applications of electronic publishing in museums includes the following:

> **Conservation.** Electronic museum collection catalogs can include more conservation documentation than previously possible in print versions. SFMOMA's Rauschenberg Research Project provides worldwide access to scholarly research and documentation including the back sides of paintings, conservation reports, and informational videos relating to artworks by Robert Rauschenberg in SFMOMA's permanent collection: go.nmc.org/rau.

> **Exhibitions and Collections.** Museum of Fine Arts, Boston brings their instrument collection to life with an e-book for the iPad. Users can see and hear 100 musical instruments of the museum's collection of 1,100, played by musicians in video clips and audio samples. The instruments featured vary from the ancient Greek trumpet and the South Indian lute to the modern American lap steel guitar: go.nmc.org/musical.

> **Marketing and Communications.** The Oakland Museum of California (OMCA) offers a free digital magazine app that is regularly updated with previews of exhibitions and videos of artists and community activists. In addition to museum-specific media, the OMCA app features interactive maps of local sites and parks, and behind-the-scenes images of collections from partner museums: go.nmc.org/omca.

Electronic Publishing in Practice

The following links provide examples of electronic publishing in use in museums:

Catalyst Magazine
go.nmc.org/denmus
The Denver Museum of Nature & Science offers its bi-monthly online publication, *Catalyst*, to museum patrons for free. The electronic magazine includes information on events, programs, and exhibitions that are shareable via Facebook, Twitter, and Pinterest with optimized links for easy web surfing.

College Art Association
go.nmc.org/caa
The Andrew W. Mellon Foundation is sponsoring the College Art Association to develop, publish, and disseminate a code of best practices for fair use in the creation and curation of artworks and scholarly publishing in the visual arts. This will help artists and art historians in securing rights for reproducing works of art electronically or in hard copy.

DallasSITES
go.nmc.org/dmg
The Dallas Museum of Art's digital publication *DallasSITES: A Developing Art Scene, Postwar to Present* traces the development of the contemporary art scene in seven neighborhoods of the city through images, chapter essays, and scholarly pieces. This publication explores the history of over 150 commercial galleries and non-profit organizations in North Texas from the mid-1950s.

Index Magazine
go.nmc.org/harvart
Earlier this year, the Harvard Art Museums launched the digital counterpart to *Index Magazine*, a resource with articles and interviews about their collections. Included on the website are opportunities to interact with museum personnel through events such as "Ask a Curator Day," wherein several curators answer questions from the public via Twitter.

MetPublications
go.nmc.org/metro
The Metropolitan Museum of Art has launched its collection of MetPublications, which offers access to books, bulletins, and journals from the past five decades in addition to 375 free art books and catalogs. Current books on the market can be previewed through the site, while out-of-print books are made available through print-on-demand.

Played in Britain
go.nmc.org/publ
The Victoria and Albert Museum's "Played in Britain: Modern Theatre in 100 Plays" iPad app guides the viewer through six decades of British theater history with production photographs, original script extracts, and audio clips.

For Further Reading

The following articles and resources are recommended for those who wish to learn more about electronic publishing.

Building an Interpretive Technology Strategy from Zero (Video)
go.nmc.org/ittt
(Koven Smith, *New Media Consortium*, 1 October 2013.) A museum technologist explains how to use the free syndication tool If This Then That to add smart capabilities to a digital publication that make it interactive but self-sufficient.

Create Once, Publish Everywhere — Reusing Museum Collection Content
go.nmc.org/cope
(Paul Rowe, *Collections and their Connections*, 7 June 2013.) A developer for a museum software company describes the content management strategy known as "Create Once, Publish Everywhere," which is currently being implemented by National Public Radio. Rowe applies this strategy to the museum world in an effort to help institutions reuse collection information online.

The Future is Now: Getty Voices Looks Back on OSCI and Towards the Future of Museum Digital Publishing
go.nmc.org/neely
(Liz Neely, *Museum Digital Publishing Bliki*, 14 August 2013.) In this article, the Director of Digital Information and Access at the Art Institute of Chicago highlights the importance of digital publishing based on the perspective of the Getty Foundation's Anne Helmreich. One of her main points is that there must be a community of digital scholarly publishers who contribute to collective knowledge by sharing experiences at conferences and working with developer partners, so that electronic publishing can progress.

The Power of Well-Considered Publishing: Graphite from the IMA
go.nmc.org/graph
(Greg Albers, *Digital Publishing*, 4 April 2013.) Three compelling features of the Indianapolis Museum of Art's GRAPHITE catalog include navigation links at the top of the book, installation shots from the actual physical show to serve as a record of the in-house show, and the ease of watching video within the publication.

The Rise of the Multimedia Authoring Platform
go.nmc.org/multi
(Rich Shivener, *Publisher's Weekly*, 1 February 2013.) Multimedia authoring tools and publishers are making it easier than ever for companies and organizations to produce digital publications that include audio, video, image, animations, and 3D models. The author examines the new generation of publishers including iBooks Author, Vook, and Inkling, and evaluates their approach to this emergent market.

Location-Based Services
Time-to-Adoption Horizon: Two to Three Years

Location-based services (LBS) provide content that is dynamically customized according to the user's location. These services are commonly delivered to mobile devices; cellular tower coordinates are often refined with GPS data to ensure a high level of accuracy in locating mobile devices. New technologies will extend that capability into buildings and interior spaces with remarkable accuracy. Current common applications for location-based services include advertising, news, social networking, and similar services. In the commercial realm, location-based services have become an almost transparent way to generate actions triggered by a user's interest data and matched to his or her location. The next and most compelling development for location-based services is the prospect of indoor geolocation, which could provide visitors with very specific information tailored to their exact location within a building, allowing fine-tuned information or services to be accessed that are very specific to where they are, not only relative to the planet's surface, but in 3D space, so that even different floors of a building can be identified.

Overview

Location-based services digitally pinpoint the precise physical position of an object or individual through WiFi and cellular networks; what makes this topic especially compelling is what the technology does with that information, including mapping efficient routes for travel and making recommendations on museums and exhibits to visit through mobile applications. Because smartphones and tablets automatically include GPS and an array of sensors, LBS enables a frictionless communication stream between people and their locations — a stream that can inform a host of mobile services and applications.

While the category is not entirely new, what has made it a topic of growing interest is its seamless integration with the tools people already commonly use, particularly social networks. Over the past few years, museums have become avid and particularly creative users of social media, making them naturally poised to leverage location-based technologies.

Today, when a user signs up for a new social network, such as Instagram or Facebook, they immediately receive a prompt asking whether the platform has permission to access their current location. In fact, some social networks' entire premise is based on location information. FourSquare, while not new, may be the most well-known example. Over the past several years it has become one of the most enduring applications in the social media space, rewarding users for checking in to places via their mobile devices. Businesses — including museums — have taken a cue from these virtual exchanges and begun giving discounts or special offers to people who tag, check in, or acknowledge the establishment across a plethora of social networks. Location-based services traverse and connect the digital and physical realms more seamlessly than ever before.

When coupled with big data and analytics on people's habits and movements — whether in or outdoors — this same concept can be taken a step further past notions of size and space and onto methods for tailoring the content that is delivered, based on people's interests. The future of location-based services is ultimately less about devices being able to discern where an individual is and more about pushing out helpful information to them before they even ask for it. That is to say, a smartphone knows if its owner has been to several history museums and can use that data to provide recommendations for further exploration.

Apple's recent purchase of two location intelligence startups that specialize in indoor GPS and crowdsourced data, Locationary and WiFiSLAM, signals a new direction for location-based services, with major applications for large museums. Location-based services are now positioned to help people better understand their environments and even contribute their own measurements in an effort to map the entire world, inside and out.

Relevance for Museum Education and Interpretation

Location-based services promise to provide museum visitors with easy access to customized educational experiences. Recently, museums have begun to respond to patrons

> Location-based services promise to provide museum visitors with easy access to customized educational experiences.

bringing their own mobile devices by providing free access to WiFi throughout their public spaces. While providing wayfinding and digital interpretive materials on mobile devices through WiFi triangulation is at the core of the latest location-based services advancements, there is further potential to personalize the individual's experience while moving within or around a museum.

Although a number of experiments are being conducted with various internal positioning systems such as Bluetooth beacons, locative LED, and active RFID, the development of WiFi triangulation to provide location-based services directly to a user's handheld device is a key strategy. At the Art Institute of Chicago (AIC), the major initiatives of offering reliable connectivity and indoor positioning have ushered in a new way to experience the nearly 150-year-old institution. Over the course of several years, the AIC retrofitted its galleries to provide WiFi in almost all of the public spaces for educational benefit. By carefully planning the placement of WiFi access points, the museum was also able to gauge a visitor's location reliably within a 30-foot radius and guide them to a selected number of artworks with associated digital assets.

The social dimension of location-based services is poised to see substantial growth in the next two to three years within the museum sector. The interplay between social media and physical space through earlier mobile apps like Foursquare and Yelp, and most recently though Locationary and Waze, has initiated a type of engagement where individuals build communities around physical locations. At the deCordova Sculpture Park and Museum, for example, artist Halsey Burgund leveraged the site-specific nature of the sculpture park in her audio installation *Scapes*. Through Roundware, a location sensitive audio platform, museum visitors navigated through the park and encountered sounds in the form of different musical instruments and melodies on their mobile devices. Additionally, visitors were encouraged to engage with the artwork by recording their observations and listening to recordings that other visitors contributed.

Because museums generally have major presences in both online and physical spaces, the increasing ability to accurately pinpoint the location of an individual provides museums with the opportunity to make these two spaces interact more meaningfully than ever before. Under the concept of Geo-fencing, a museum's website would know where a visitor was and would localize information and push it to them. For example, a museum's website would push information to a mobile device about the visiting hours and admission fee if a user was within the vicinity of the institution's entrance, or collections information if he or she was standing directly in front of an artifact.

While many location-based services projects are currently underway, this topic falls on the mid-term horizon mainly because of the costs related to retrofitting galleries with the appropriate technologies and accuracy limitations of current indoor positioning systems.

A sampling of applications of location-based services in museums includes the following:

> **Exhibitions and Collections.** The Timken Museum of Art launched a prototype of a mobile app that serves information about artworks based on visitors' location within the galleries. A PlaceSticker device is assigned to each artwork, sending low-power radio signals to visitors' smartphones and tablets to determine their location and deliver content: go.nmc.org/timken.

> **Marketing and Communications.** With Foursquare now integrated into the Instagram app, museums can use this tool to gather location-based information from geo-tagged photos that visitors share on the platform. By analyzing patrons' behaviors, museums can gain insight into the most popular features of a particular exhibition or event: go.nmc.org/nitro.

> **Visitor Services and Accessibility.** The Royal BC Museum in Canada worked with the company WiFarer to create an app that enables each visitor to personalize their museum exploration based on a map that pinpoints visitors and guides them to preferred artworks and collections. The location-based content adds more in-depth interaction to each exhibit: go.nmc.org/rbc.

Location-Based Services in Practice

The following links provide examples of location-based services in use in museums and other settings:

ByteLight
go.nmc.org/byte
LED light bulbs from the Massachusetts-based company ByteLight send location-specific information to visitors in the Museum of Science, Boston by interacting with their devices' camera, using signals that are invisible to the human eye.

Fernbank Museum App
go.nmc.org/fer
Atlanta's Fernbank Museum of Natural History's app tracks visitors' locations once they enter the museum to deliver a combination of audio, video, touchscreen interactives, animation, sketchbook activities, and question-and-answer challenges, while also encouraging sharing of the experience through social media platforms.

Indoor GPS at AIC
go.nmc.org/indo
The Art Institute of Chicago uses an indoor GPS system powered by Meridian to take visitors on customized tours organized by occasion, theme, collection, and time. Each tour showcases six to ten works of art, with descriptions and turn-by-turn directions.

Kew Gardens App
go.nmc.org/kew
The Royal Botanic Garden, Kew, has developed an Android app that uses GPS and WiFi technology to offer visitors new ways for wayfinding and interpretation. The app guides visitors over 300 acres of outdoor space and through three glass houses, along with offering interactive media about surrounding plants and trees.

Pocket Ranger
go.nmc.org/chal
ParksbyNature Network LLC's "Pocket Ranger" apps invite users to embark on geochallenges, visiting as many of the California state parks and state recreation areas as possible over the next year using their GPS-enabled apps to map out each trip. Participants earn points by visiting state parks and recreation areas, with easy-to-reach parks yielding five points and more distant locales garnering them 20 points.

Wikimedia's Nearby
go.nmc.org/nearby
The Wikimedia Foundation introduced a new "Nearby" page to operate in conjunction with its mobile site, surfacing articles based on a user's location. It is also an easy way for Wikimedia editors to upload photo content for entries that are in need of images or improve articles on topics in close proximity.

For Further Reading

The following articles and resources are recommended for those who wish to learn more about location-based services:

Baseball's Beacon Trials Hint at Apple's Location Revolution
go.nmc.org/ibe
(Roger Cheng, *CNet*, 28 September 2013.) A new feature of iOS 7, iBeacon, improves the capability of location-based services for the iPhone. MLB.com recently tested its capabilities at Citi Field where visitors received a welcome message and discounts as they entered the premises.

History as an App(arition)
go.nmc.org/hist
(Rhodri Marsden, *ioL travel*, 15 August 2013.) The City of York Hologram Tour is an app backed by the York City Council that displays holograms of actors in costume explaining specific York locations when the visitor arrives at each point. The author of this article describes the experience of using the app, and how it could be amplified in the future when users are able to access it with Google Glass or other wearable devices.

Location Based Guidance Services in a Museum Environment: Deployment Issues and a Proposed Architectural Approach
go.nmc.org/guid
(Nikolaos Konstantinou et al., *Academia.edu*, accessed 1 October 2013.) This paper examines the requirements for deploying location-based guidance services in museums that can react to contextual triggers. This service is built as an open, modular platform with reusable components and interfaces for supporting different types of devices, including Java- and Bluetooth-enabled smartphones.

Mapping and Location-Based Geo Services
go.nmc.org/geo
(Yu-Tzu Chiu, *IEEE Spectrum*, 20 November 2012.) Engineers from STMicroelectronics and CSR modified a Google Nexus One smartphone to integrate an indoor navigation module for visitors to the Museum of Contemporary Art in Taipei. As a visitor approaches an object, its corresponding icon pops up on their device's screen so they can click on it for more information.

This Startup's Cheap Sensors Could Create an OS for Everyday Life
go.nmc.org/star
(Kyle Vanhemert, *WIRED*, 7 August 2013.) Estimote is an attempt to build an operating system for the physical world out of a network of cheap, low-energy transmitters. The creators envision seamless location awareness that will allow interactions and experiences that are tightly integrated with real places, from parks to parking lots.

Why Wifi Networks are the Future of Location-Based Mobile
go.nmc.org/meri
(Nick Farina, nfarina.com, May 2013.) The company Meridian helped the American Museum of Natural History build its "AMNH Explorer" app, which uses a device's WiFi signal to calculate the visitor's position within the museum. The author believes that WiFi is the key to the advancement of location-based services, specifically indoor GPS.

Natural User Interfaces
Time-to-Adoption Horizon: Four to Five Years

It is already common to interact with devices entirely by using natural movements and gestures. The iPad, iPhone and iPod Touch, Xbox Kinect, Nintendo Wii, the new class of "smart TVs," and a host of other devices built with natural user interfaces (NUIs) accept input in the form of taps, swipes, and other ways of touching; hand and arm motions; body movement; and increasingly, natural language. These are the first in a growing array of devices that recognize and interpret natural physical gestures as a means of control. New technologies already extend these capabilities, and even read the emotional state of the user via voice and microexpressions of the face. Already in prototype are new forms of screen technologies that will convey highly detailed sensations of texture, and provide natural tactile feedback. What makes natural user interfaces especially interesting this year is the burgeoning high fidelity of systems that understand gestures, facial expressions, and their nuances, as well as the convergence of gesture-sensing technology with voice recognition and new forms of tactile feedback like electrovibration, which allows users to interact in an almost natural fashion, with gesture, expression, and voice communicating their intentions to devices.

Overview

Although natural user interfaces were largely popularized with the launch of the iPhone and its touchscreen in 2007, the technology itself was not new at the time. Discussions around the development of interfaces beyond command line interface (CLI) and graphical user interface (GUI) started in the 1970s and 80s when Steve Mann, widely regarded as the father of wearable computing, began experimenting with human-machine interactions. From his work, the idea of natural user interfaces was born, along with the potential for scientists and designers to adapt this innovation to new technologies. Perhaps more so than other learning environments, museum spaces are naturally conducive to incorporating large-scale NUIs into exhibits and collections.

Humans interacting with computers in a natural user interface are not always conscious of the framework because their gestures seamlessly influence their experience, mimicking the real world far more than an interface based on metaphors like commands and graphics. The appeal of this innovation is that a museum patron can experience information presented in a variety of modes without the distance that traditional interfaces impose; in other words, nothing gets in the way between the user and the information. Visitors have the opportunity to truly interact with the artworks.

These types of NUIs can have profound effects on learners within the museum realm. For example, children using multi-touch walls and displays adapt to the mechanism quite naturally, which has increased support for using smartphones, tablets, and Microsoft Kinect for learning. Natural user interfaces also cater to blind and deaf patrons, along with people with autism, dyslexia, or other disabilities, making it easier for the user to communicate and learn through touch, voice, and other gestures.

While touchscreens and video and motion sensor products, including Nintendo Wii and Microsoft Kinect, have now been around for years, they have been critical benchmarks in the path to fostering completely natural interactions. Electrovibration is the next step in making the connections as authentic as possible. First discovered in 1954, this technology refers to the process when a finger is dragged across a conductive, insulated surface, creating an electrostatic force that results in a palpable sensation of touch and texture. Applied to mobile devices, the phenomenon of electrically induced tactile sensation is expected to herald the next evolution of touchscreen technology, offering the potential to feel the museum works being viewed.

Finnish company Senseg is at the forefront of applying this haptic technology to smartphone and tablets, and Disney Research is also exploring electrovibration. Senseg's electrovibration technology can be applied to any touch interface to create what they call "feel screens," where users can feel textures on the screen. The future of "feel screen"-enhanced devices offers many possibilities for deeper interaction with educational content, and with it an accessibility that caters to users with physical and mental disabilities — making it a particularly exciting technology for museums.

Speech-to-speech translation is also adding more traction around the topic of natural user interfaces. It is already common to see people interacting with voice-activated virtual assistants on their mobile devices. The next steps include new technologies like automatic translation engines — Microsoft engineers have already demoed software that can synthesize an individual's voice in another language, from English to Mandarin. Progress in these machine learning technologies points to a world where people can connect to content — and each other — more effectively.

Relevance for Museum Education and Interpretation

Natural user interfaces render technology transparent and are transforming the way museums can present their collections and exhibitions, as well as the way visitors interact with museums and their content. The desire to touch and manipulate collections is inherent in museum audiences, and although preservation and conservation issues may limit interactions with the authentic work, NUIs can compensate by allowing the visitor the experience of tactile contact or the ability to rotate an object in space. As new user interfaces become increasingly mainstream, museums have the opportunity to use these sorts of developments to create entirely new forms of interpretation and presentation.

Measuring 40 feet wide, the Collection Wall at the Cleveland Museum of Art is the largest multi-touchscreen in the United States, and it stands at the leading edge of thinking about how visitors can interact with a museum's collection in a fundamentally different way. Multi-touch technology enables patrons to move, select, and sort multimedia assets for open-ended exploration in a very intuitive manner. The Collection Wall demonstrates this at a scale never before seen in a museum space.

In addition to multi-touch technology, motion-sensing input devices are radically transforming how museum guests engage with collections. At the New Mexico Museum of Art, marionettes once considered too fragile to even be exhibited are given a new life. After creating digital surrogates of selected marionettes from the museum's collection, students from New Mexico Highlands University are using Kinect to enable visitors to use natural hand gestures to see how these objects function, for the first time in decades.

Yet another dimension of NUIs is beginning to play out in the gallery itself, as artists push the boundaries of this new set of tools to create large-scale immersive environments. In the summer of 2013, the Museum of Modern Art presented the Rain Room, an art installation where visitors could stop simulated rain drops from falling on them by moving about a room outfitted with sensors that recognized the presence of objects and movement.

Emerging sensing technologies, like the electrovibration project headed by Disney Research, could open up a whole new world of interpretation with the ability to understand the rich spatial dimensionality of an object through digital means without having to worry about damaging a fragile object. By generating the simulations of edges, protrusions, and bumps through frictional forces between finger and screen, museum visitors will be able to experience the heavily impastoed surface of a Van Gogh work in an entirely new way.

Discovery-based learning opportunities for museums are steadily increasing since this technology first appeared in the *NMC Horizon Report:2012 Museum Edition*, where it was also in the far-term horizon. Despite many experiments, NUIs are still four to five years away because few museums have the in-house skills to develop this kind of technology for educational purposes. Nonetheless, the future for natural user interfaces is promising as special exhibitions begin to build museums' inventories of devices, along with the expertise to use NUIs in more imaginative ways.

A sampling of applications of natural user interfaces in museums and other settings includes the following:

> **Exhibitions and Collections.** The "Spotlight on The Antinoe Veil" exhibition at the Louvre uses Microsoft Kinect's gesture-based sensor technology that enables visitors to interact with an ancient artifact. The Greek tapestry, which is delicate and difficult to decipher, can now be manipulated by museum patrons in its digital form: go.nmc.org/louvre.

> **Marketing and Communications.** The Children's Medical Center in Dallas has an Interactive Donor Wall where each supporter's name is represented in a bubble that users can manipulate with their gestures: go.nmc.org/dono.

> **Visitor Services and Accessibility.** The Manchester Museum developed a way to let blind and partially sighted visitors touch digital models of their exhibits, using a haptic device called a Probos. Visitors sit in front of a device with a screen and a stylus connected via a mechanical arm and the screen displays a 3D model of an object such as a pot, bone, or statue. go.nmc.org/fee.

Natural User Interfaces in Practice

The following links provide examples of natural user interfaces in use in museums and other settings:

3D Bird Animation and Gesture Recognition
go.nmc.org/nati
Unified Field built the "Dance, Dance Evolution" game for National Geographic's "Birds of Paradise" exhibit using a Kinect sensor to allow players to enact movements that control a virtual 3D bird as it performs real mating dance rituals.

The Baumann Marionettes Go 3D
go.nmc.org/mari
Highland University programming students are using Kinect to create 3D representations of around 75 of Gustave Baumann's marionettes that are owned by the New Mexico Museum of Art. Users will be able to virtually manipulate the marionettes through hand gestures, and the 3D marionette models will also be available in the museum's online database.

Nocturnal Animal Senses
go.nmc.org/natu
The "Nocturnal Animal Senses" exhibit at the Natural Science Museum Complex in Romania demonstrates to visitors how animals thrive at night. The installation is composed of various screens of all sizes that, when touched, reveal information about an animal's environment, hunting habits, and how they navigate in darkness.

Shop Life
go.nmc.org/shoplife
In New York City, the Tenement Museum's "Shop Life" installation is a 25-foot interactive tabletop that provides visitors with the opportunity to explore three immigrant business scenarios from the 1860s to the 1970s. Stories are shared through images, video, and audio.

Sports Hall
go.nmc.org/pero
"Sports Hall," an exhibit at Perot Museum, invites visitors to throw a fastball, kick a soccer ball, or turn cartwheels while a high-speed camera captures it so visitors can review their own movements to learn about motion, how body positioning affects speed, and other factors of sports science.

THINK
go.nmc.org/thinkex
With the aid of a media field of seven-foot

interactive touchscreens, the "THINK" exhibit at Schenectady Museum presents visitors with a hands-on way to view the history of technological innovations. The technology behind the exhibit is powered by IBM.

Universe of Sound
go.nmc.org/univ
The "Universe of Sound" installation at the London Science Museum incorporates video rooms, instruments, and pods with 3D motion sensors to create an immersive experience in which visitors learn what it takes to be a musician as well as how to be a conductor in a philharmonic orchestra.

Wearing Many Hats (Video)
go.nmc.org/hats
At The Peabody Essex Museum in Massachusetts, an interactive station called "Wearing Many Hats" encourages visitors to explore generations of hat design. Using touchscreens to capture photos of themselves, visitors scroll through various hats until they find one they like. They can then email or print the photo of themselves wearing the virtual hat.

For Further Reading

The following articles and resources are recommended for those who wish to learn more about natural user interfaces.

5 Lessons In UI Design, from a Breakthrough Museum
go.nmc.org/bre
(Cliff Kuang, *Fast Company*, 6 March 2013.) The Cleveland Museum of Art unveiled a series of revamped galleries to connect visitors with art in a way that emphasizes the content without letting the technology overshadow it. For example, a virtual easel sits in front of a Jackson Pollock painting, loaded with tools that approximate Pollock's own, so visitors can create their own drip painting and compare it to the real thing.

How Helsinki-Based Startup Senseg Creates Touchscreens You Can Feel
go.nmc.org/helsin
(Stephen Kelly, *WIRED*, 11 April 13.) Finnish company Senseg has produced a thin durable material that uses an ultra-low electrical current to create an attractive force that allows the user to feel textures, edges, and vibrations. They plan to "haptify" the whole user interface for smartphones and tablet prototypes.

Leap Motion: 1 million App Downloads in 3 Weeks
go.nmc.org/leapmo
(John Koetsier, *VentureBeat*, 12 August 2013.) Leap Motion created a keyboard-free computer controller that is 200 times more accurate than the Microsoft Kinect, and allows users to control their computers with midair gestures. Three weeks after their launch, Leap Motion saw over one million downloads of its apps and 25,000 downloads of their software development kit.

Lighting Solutions React to Become More Personal
go.nmc.org/light
(*PSFK*, 22 September 2013.) Richmond Park in London installed a LumiMotion lighting system that is able to detect when a person approaches a light at night and increases brightness accordingly. After the person passes, the lights decrease in intensity to save energy.

Medical Museum Seeks Bucks for Touch Screen Walls, Other High-Tech Goodies
go.nmc.org/doyle
(Lizzie Schiffman, *DNAinfo Chicago*, 8 April 2013.) A computer scientist and museum professional is working on a prototype for a "museum without walls" at the National Museum of Health and Medicine that will inform the construction of a satellite institution in Chicago. For the new space, he envisions floor-to-ceiling interactive screens that can be customized according to the installation or event.

New Disney Technology Can Add Texture to Completely Smooth Touchscreen
go.nmc.org/distech
(PBS, 7 October 2013.) Disney researchers in Pittsburgh have applied electrovibration to smooth touchscreens, resulting in a textured sensation that mimics ridges, depths, and other three dimensional experiences. The new technology also leverages research on how the brain is fooled into perceiving bumps by the stretching of the skin on the fingertip.

Preservation and Conservation Technologies
Time-to-Adoption Horizon: Four to Five Years

As long as there have been museums, their mission has been to preserve and conserve our collective cultural heritage. Preservation refers to the protection of important objects, artifacts, and documents; conservation is the science of maintaining objects in as close to their original form as possible. For both actions, there is a need to ensure that the processes are reversible so that future generations can undo the work or make revisions. As technology evolves, archivists and conservators have encountered a steady stream of new challenges in both of these tasks. Digital objects can be as delicate as ancient objects, requiring special care, and changing technologies put these digital items at great risk. Cultural works that are time-based add a level of complexity in the quest for preservation, due to the added consideration of the artist's intent, context, or movement. Understanding and preserving how media is intended to be experienced while maintaining the integrity of its cultural identity encompasses a number of considerations such as conservation ethics, legal agreements, availability of mechanical and/or digital materials, and historical scholarship. While large museums have long employed specialists in artifact preservation, today new professionals are needed who understand digital and time-based media, and can address preservation and conservation challenges not only from physical, but artistic, cultural, engineering, electronic, and other multi-disciplinary perspectives.

Overview

Although the terms preservation and conservation are often used interchangeably, they are distinct in their purposes; preservation is meant to protect and/or retard the natural disintegrative properties of artifacts, and the act of conservation is intended to stabilize and restore artifacts in so far as that is possible. When practiced concurrently, they future-proof both physical and digital media, while keeping the original meaning behind the objects intact. Preservation and conservation technologies appear here on the far-term horizon, but they are not new topics for educational and cultural

> **Aside from maintaining the physical state of this media, a major concern is ensuring that the process of the conservation does not eclipse the meaning behind it.**

institutions. The position of these intertwined topics is an acknowledgement of the challenges involved in protecting and restoring an exponentially increasing number of artifacts — whether analog, digitally native, or time-based in format.

Over the past several decades, a number of key organizations have developed models and standards that continue to shape the practices of preservation. In 1994, the Research Libraries Group and the Commission on Preservation and Access formed the Task Force on Archiving of Digital Information, which ultimately developed a national system of digital archives for long-term storage, and were the first to present digital repositories as part of the solution. To standardize the practice of preservation, they created the Open Archival

Information System, a landmark method for authenticating digital documents and objects, which the Online Computer Library Center built upon after the millennium. This framework encompasses the technical aspects of the workflow, from the ingesting of digital objects to data management and access, along with recommending five types of metadata to accompany each object: reference information, provenance, context, fixity, and representation.

In the museum realm, digital preservation calls for a new type of staff member with skills that span hardware technologies, file structures and formats, storage media, electronic processors and chips, and more, blending the training of an electrical engineer with the skills of an inventor and a computer scientist. Decoding content and recovering material from devices or storage media that may not have been used for decades requires equipment and knowledge

> **Museums are entering an era where the number of digital artifacts is quickly surpassing that of physical objects within a museum.**

that few museums have, outside those specializing in computer technology.

While preservation has largely been an ongoing pursuit for archivists, scientists, and libraries, the act of conservation is perhaps most needed in the museum sector, where millions of physical artworks demand constant attention from staff to remain stable and displayable. Furthermore, art installations that incorporate audio, video, moving elements, or require human interactions have added another layer of complexity, blending the physical with the digital. Aside from maintaining the physical state of this media, a major concern is ensuring that the process of the conservation does not eclipse the meaning behind it. This raises the need for curators to consult with the artists, or review the records of deceased artists to make sure that the original intent is interpreted as closely as possible.

Museums across the world also have large collections of electronic media objects, each representing unique challenges from a preservation and conservation standpoint, including antiquated operating systems, hardware, and computer programs. Both optical and magnetic storage fade over time, corrupting once-readable data merely through the passage of time. Furthermore, these challenges still do not address the issues of file formats and run-time use of the files, once they can be accessed via the appropriate hardware. While future technologies cannot be fully foreseen, the fact that conversations about preservation and conservation are increasingly taking place is an indication that they are poised to become better understood and executed over the next four to five years.

Relevance for Museum Education and Interpretation

Museums are entering an era where the number of digital artifacts is quickly surpassing that of physical objects within a museum. Objects created with outdated technologies are at risk of being estranged from the creator's original intent. Although preservation and conservation are of critical importance to the health and educational importance of museum collections, understanding the specific strategies and technologies needed to remedy these issues in museums and the amount of staff trained to address them is an evolving challenge.

University library programs are pioneering the new field of digital curation, and helping to train a generation of future museum staff to address preserving and restoring the most problematic time-based and digital materials. In addition to developing an understanding of archival theory and metadata standards, students are working directly with contemporary artists to determine the best ways to preserve the integrity of artworks for generations to come.

The conservation of time-based media poses a particular challenge for art museums because these objects often consist of special mechanical components or use technologies or formats that are obsolete, combined with a specific intention. For example, deceased video installation artist and sculptor Nam June Paik was best known for creating artworks using cathode ray tube monitors and analog television signals. The continued maintenance and presentation of Paik's artworks have required museum conservators and preparators to make decisions on how to present them, which often requires deviating from his intent — directly affecting the interpretation of his objects.

While museums have been slow to take up formal strategies and policies for securing and repairing their digital and time-based collections from deterioration, archives and libraries are hard at work on possible technological solutions. Currently the Library of Congress is conducting research on historic sound recordings that have been damaged or are deteriorating. This investigation inspired recent MacArthur Fellow and audio preservationist Carl Haber to create a system using high gigapixel images and specialized image processing to calculate the sound that an analog record would make. In 2012 the cultural significance of his work was highlighted as his technique enabled individuals to hear Alexander Graham Bell's voice for the very first time.

The introduction of preservation and conservation technologies in the *NMC Horizon Report* is significant because it shows that museums are becoming more broadly aware that they are facing major problems in the imminent future if the intricacies of the topic are not more widely understood and acted upon in the field. There are few known initiatives to serve as best practice models for conservation and preservation efforts, however, this topic's placement in the far-term horizon reflects an increased focus from museums.

A sampling of applications for preservation and conservation technologies in museums includes the following:

> **Exhibitions and Collections.** The Dallas Museum of Art is opening its new Paintings Conservation Studio as part of the museum's initiative to establish a more comprehensive in-house conservation program. The Paintings Conservation Studio features state-of-the-art technology — including a digital x-ray system — and will serve as a center for study and treatment of works of art as well as research into cutting-edge conservation methodologies. Visitors will be able to see into the studio through a glass wall to observe the daily activity: go.nmc.org/pai.

> **Marketing and Communications.** Museum blogs are increasingly featuring content from conservation departments as a way to provide behind-the-scenes access to rarely seen activities. The British Museum's blog features scientific images and a YouTube video about the work being done to conserve and display the Beau Street Hoard, a collection of Roman coins: go.nmc.org/beau.

> **Visitor Services and Accessibility.** A media archiving project called XFR STN at the New Museum of Contemporary Art is digitizing and disseminating digitally-native materials whose formats have become obsolete in a publically operating exhibition on archive.org, an Internet library offering permanent access for a variety of audiences, including people with disabilities: go.nmc.org/newm.

Preservation and Conservation Technologies in Practice

The following links provide examples of preservation and conservation technologies in use that have direct implications for museums:

Australia's Oldest Culture Enters the Digital Age
go.nmc.org/samuseum
Remote Aboriginal communities will have

access to documented family histories, photos, and artifacts dating back to 1830 as the South Australian Museum digitizes the largest collection of its kind in the world. Some items in the collection will be made available internationally, while other sections will be restricted to ensure their cultural sensitivity.

CHIN's Digital Preservation Toolkit
go.nmc.org/chi
The Canadian Heritage Information Network (CHIN) recently conducted a survey among their members to identify digital preservation issues facing museums, and will soon release its Digital Preservation Toolkit, a suite of documents that offer concrete steps to identify the potential risk and impact of lost material and how to get started in the development of preservation policies, plans, and procedures.

High-Resolution Digital Slides of Einstein's Brain
go.nmc.org/ape
Aperio ePathology has digitized over 550 slides of Einstein's brain that were originally donated to the National Museum of Health and Medicine in Maryland. This will enable researchers, scientists, and enthusiasts around the world to view the original slides prepared by Dr. Thomas Harvey, the pathologist who conducted the autopsy of Albert Einstein in 1955.

Media Conservation Lab at the Guggenheim
go.nmc.org/gug
The Guggenheim launched a Media Conservation Lab to assess and monitor the image and sound content of time-based media works that include video, film, slide, audio or computer-based technologies and therefore have duration as a dimension.

Robot Helps Restore Works
go.nmc.org/rest
A robot in Madrid's Reina Sofia Museum scans artworks by snapping photos that reveal cracks, scratches, creases, underlying preparatory sketches, and all subsequent touch-ups that would be otherwise undetectable to the human eye. The robot can be controlled by a computer from a remote location and work around the clock.

Time-Based Media Conservation at Tate
go.nmc.org/tat
Tate's time-based media department is responsible for a number of conservation activities including documenting artist intention via interviews, along with planning and preparing for future obsolescence of the technologies incorporated in each work.

Walters Art Museum Manuscript Collection at Stanford
go.nmc.org/walt
Walters Art Museum and Stanford University Libraries are working together to preserve more than 100,000 high-resolution images of unique medieval manuscripts in a format that allows scholars to use digital handling tools to analyze the manuscripts.

Wolfsonian Museum Goes Digital
go.nmc.org/wol
In order to make online catalog searches productive, the Wolfsonian Museum in Florida has undertaken the process of photographing the museum's more than 120,000 objects and entering in accompanying data, including the name of the artist or manufacturer, the year and place of origin, and the original media from which it was created.

For Further Reading

The following articles and resources are recommended for those who wish to learn more about preservation and conservation technologies:

Best of Both Worlds(PDF)
go.nmc.org/smin
(G. Wayne Clough, Smithsonian Institution, 2013.) The Smithsonian Institution's free 77-page e-book covers their process of digitizing over 14 million objects from their massive collections. The author illuminates how museums are challenged to evolve with the digital age despite the high cost of digitizing

collections.

Conservation and Digital Imaging - Part 1
go.nmc.org/osulab
(Amy McCroy, *University Libraries*, 18 June 2013.) Conservators at The Digital Imaging Unit of the OSU Libraries provide an inside look at what processes are involved in the repair, stabilization, and eventual digitization of books, manuscripts, and artifacts of cultural heritage. Every piece that is digitized is stored in OSU's Knowledge Bank where it can be accessed online.

Science Benefits Art Preservation
go.nmc.org/ben
(Greg Flakus, *Voice of America*, 30 September 2013.) A painting found in someone's attic in Europe was established to be a newly discovered work by Vincent Van Gogh after paint samples were taken from other Van Gogh artworks, and imaging tests were used to compare threads in the canvases.

Towards a Digital Preservation Policy for Museums
go.nmc.org/digsig
(Madeline Sheldon, *The Signal*, 13 June 2013.) A museum researcher describes the current climate of digital preservation as a field in its nascent stage for cultural institutions, with libraries and archives at the forefront of digital preservation planning. She points to time-based media preservation initiatives by Rhizome, the Guggenheim, and Tate that are shaping the strategies other museums can refer to when planning their own preservation policies.

When Artworks Crash: Restorers Face Digital Test
go.nmc.org/digart
(Melena Ryzik, *The New York Times*, 9 June 2013.) When the Whitney Museum of American Art acquired one of the first Internet-made artworks, a piece called "The World's First Collaborative Sentence," conservators were faced with the conceptual debate of how to maintain the work's integrity although its medium — code from the 1990s — was obsolete. Cultural institutions will have to develop specialists in this area as new, digital artworks continue to emerge.

When Homework is Real Work: Digital Curation Students Help Preserve Media Art
go.nmc.org/cur
(Jon Ippolito, *Still Water Blog*, 18 August 2013.) Students in the University of Maine's Digital Curation program are learning how to use free online tools such as Variable Media Questionnaire to record opinions of artists about how to conserve creative works when their current mediums become obsolete. This tool is already in use by the Guggenheim and Whitney, as well as archives including the Langlois Foundation and Rhizome.org.

University library programs are pioneering the new field of digital curation, and helping to train a generation of future museum staff to address preserving and restoring the most problematic time-based and digital materials.

The NMC Horizon Project

This report is part of a longitudinal research study of emerging technologies that began in March 2002. Since that time, under the banner of the Horizon Project, the NMC and its research partners have held an ongoing series of conversations and dialogs with its advisory boards — a group that now numbers over 850 technology professionals, campus technologists, faculty leaders from colleges and universities, museum professionals, teachers and other school professionals, and representatives of leading corporations from all over the world. For more than a decade, these conversations have been mined to provide the insights on emerging technology that are published annually in the *NMC Horizon Report* series.

The NMC Horizon Project is currently in its eleventh year, dedicated to charting the landscape of emerging technologies for teaching, learning, and creative inquiry in education globally. In 2008, the NMC added to the three main *NMC Horizon Reports* a new series of regional and sector-based studies, called the *NMC Technology Outlooks,* with the dual goals of understanding how technology is being absorbed using a smaller lens, and also noting the contrasts between technology use in one area compared to another.

To date, the NMC has conducted studies of technology uptake in Australia, New Zealand, the UK, Latin America, Brazil, Singapore, and Norway, and has extended that research to Europe. In 2012, the *Technology Outlook* series was expanded to include sector analyses, and so far has documented technology uptake across STEM+ education and community, technical, and junior colleges.

The 44 members of this year's advisory board were purposefully chosen to represent a broad spectrum of the museum sector; key writers, thinkers, technologists, and futurists from museums, education, business, and industry rounded out the group. They engaged in a comprehensive review and analysis of research, articles, papers, blogs, and interviews, discussed existing applications, and brainstormed new ones, and ultimately ranked the items on the list of candidate technologies for their potential relevance to museum education and interpretation. This work took place entirely online and may be reviewed on the project wiki at museum.wiki.nmc.org.

The effort to produce the *NMC Horizon Report: 2013 Museum Edition* began in August 2013, and concluded when the report was released in November 2013, a period of just over three months. The six technologies and applications that emerged at the top of the final rankings — two per adoption horizon — are detailed in the preceding chapters.

Each of those chapters includes detailed descriptions, links to active demonstration projects, and a wide array of additional resources related to the six profiled technologies. Those profiles are the heart of the *NMC Horizon Report: 2013 Museum Edition*, and will fuel the work of the NMC Horizon Project throughout the year. To share your educational technology projects with the NMC to potentially be featured in a future *NMC Horizon Report*, the NMC Horizon Project Navigator database, or the NMC Horizon EdTech Weekly App, visit go.nmc.org/projects. For those wanting to know more about the processes used to generate the *NMC Horizon Report* series, many of which are ongoing and extend the work in the reports, we refer you to the report's final section on the research methodology.

The 44 members of this year's advisory board were purposefully chosen to represent a broad spectrum of the museum sector; key writers, thinkers, technologists, and futurists from museums, education, business, and industry rounded out the group.

Methodology

The process used to research and create the *NMC Horizon Report: 2013 Museum Edition* is very much rooted in the methods used across all the research conducted within the NMC Horizon Project. All editions in the *NMC Horizon Report* series are produced using a carefully constructed process that is informed by both primary and secondary research. Dozens of technologies, meaningful trends, and critical challenges are examined for possible inclusion in the report for each edition. Every report draws

Dozens of technologies, meaningful trends, and critical challenges are examined for possible inclusion in the report for each edition.

on the considerable expertise of an internationally renowned advisory board that first considers a broad set of important emerging technologies, challenges, and trends, and then examines each of them in progressively more detail, reducing the set until the final listing of technologies, trends, and challenges is selected.

This process takes place online, where it is captured and placed in the NMC Horizon Project wiki. The wiki is intended to be a completely transparent window onto the work of the project, and contains the entire record of the research for each of the various editions.

The section of the wiki used for the *NMC Horizon Report: 2013 Museum Edition* can be found at museum.wiki.nmc.org.

The procedure for selecting the topics in the report included a modified Delphi process now refined over years of producing the *NMC Horizon Report* series, and began with the assembly of the advisory board. The advisory board represents a wide range of backgrounds, nationalities, and interests, yet each member brings a particularly relevant expertise. Over the decade of the NMC Horizon Project research, more than 850 internationally recognized practitioners and experts have participated on project advisory boards; in any given year, a third of advisory board members are new, ensuring a flow of fresh perspectives each year. Nominations to serve on the advisory board are encouraged — see go.nmc.org/horizon-nominate.

Once the advisory board for a particular edition is constituted, their work begins with a systematic review of the literature — press clippings, reports, essays, and other materials — that pertains to emerging technology. Advisory board members are provided with an extensive set of background materials when the project begins, and are then asked to comment on them, identify those that seem especially worthwhile, and add to the set. The group discusses existing applications of emerging technology and brainstorms new ones. A key criterion for the inclusion of a topic in this edition is its potential relevance to museum education and interpretation. A carefully selected set of RSS feeds from hundreds of relevant publications ensures that background resources stay current as the project progresses. They are used to inform the thinking of the participants throughout the process.

Following the review of the literature, the advisory board engages in the central focus of the research — the research questions that are at the core of the NMC Horizon Project. These questions were designed to elicit a comprehensive listing of interesting technologies, challenges, and trends from the advisory board:

1 **Which of the key technologies catalogued in the NMC Horizon Project Listing will be most important to museum education and interpretation within the next five years?**

2 **What key technologies are missing from our list? Consider these related questions:**

> **What would you list among the established technologies that some institutions are using today that arguably *all* museums should be using broadly to support or enhance museum education and interpretation?**
> **What technologies that have a solid user base in consumer, entertainment, or other industries should museums be actively looking for ways to apply?**
> **What are the key emerging technologies you see developing to the point that museums should begin to take notice during the next four to five years?**

3 **What do you see as the key challenges related to education and interpretation that museums will face during the next five years?**

4 **What trends do you expect will have a significant impact on the ways in which museums use technologies in the service of mission-mandated goals related to education and interpretation?**

One of the advisory board's most important tasks is to answer these questions as systematically and broadly as possible, so as to ensure that the range of relevant topics is considered. Once this work is done, a process that moves quickly over just a few days, the advisory board moves to a unique consensus-building process based on an iterative Delphi-based methodology.

In the first step of this approach, the responses to the research questions are systematically ranked and placed into adoption horizons by each advisory board member using a multi-vote system that allows members to weight their selections. Each member is asked to also identify the timeframe during which they feel the technology would enter mainstream use — defined for the purpose of the project as about 20% of institutions adopting it within the period discussed. (This figure is based on the research of Geoffrey A. Moore and refers to the critical mass of adoptions needed for a technology to have a chance of entering broad use.) These rankings are compiled into a collective set of responses, and inevitably, the ones around which there is the most agreement are quickly apparent.

From the comprehensive list of technologies originally considered for any report, the 12 that emerge at the top of the initial ranking process — four per adoption horizon — are further researched and expanded. Once this "Short List" is identified, the group, working with both NMC staff and practitioners in the field, begins to explore the ways in which these twelve important technologies might be used for museum education and interpretation. A significant amount of time is spent researching real and potential applications for each of the areas that would be of interest to practitioners.

For every edition, when that work is done, each of these twelve "Short List" items is written up in the format of the *NMC Horizon Report*. With the benefit of the full picture of how the topic will look in the report, the "Short List" is then ranked yet again, this time in reverse. The six technologies and applications that emerge are those detailed in the *NMC Horizon Report*.

For additional detail on the project methodology or to review the actual instrumentation, the ranking, and the interim products behind the report, please visit museum.wiki.nmc.org.

The NMC Horizon Project:
2013 Museum Edition Advisory Board

Larry Johnson
Co-Principal Investigator
New Media Consortium
United States

Koven Smith
Co-Principal Investigator
Denver Art Museum
United States

Holly Witchey
Co-Principal Investigator
Johns Hopkins University
United States

Samantha Adams Becker
Lead Writer/Researcher
New Media Consortium
United States

Alex Freeman
Editor
MIDEA
United States

Susana Smith Bautista
University of Southern California
United States

Allegra Burnette
Museum of Modern Art (MOMA)
United States

Suse Cairns
MuseumGeek Blog
Australia

Sheila Carey
Canadian Heritage Information Network
Canada

Erin Coburn
Consultant
United States

David Dean
Museum of Texas Tech University
United States

Guy Deschenes
PhD Candidate, Museology, UQAM
Canada

Ryan Donahue
The Metropolitan Museum of Art
United States

Jennifer Foley
Cleveland Museum of Art
United States

Vivian Kung Haga
Balboa Park Online Collaborative
United States

Susan Hazan
The Israel Museum, Jerusalem
Israel

Phyllis Hecht
JHU Museum Studies
United States

Jessica Heimberg
Dallas Museum of Art
United States

Nik Honeysett
J. Paul Getty Museum of Art
United States

Lynda Kelly
Australian National Maritime Museum
Australia

Eli Kuslansky
Unified Field
United States

Rob Lancefield
Davison Art Center, Wesleyan University
United States

Miriam Langer
New Mexico Highlands University
United States

Jack Ludden
J. Paul Getty Trust
United States

Elizabeth Merritt
AAM
United States

Jonathan Munar
Art 21
United States

Mike Murawski
Portland Art Museum
United States

Liz Neely
Art Institute of Chicago
United States

Lorna O'Brien
North Lands Creative Glass /
Timespan Museum and Arts Centre
Scotland

Lori Byrd Phillips
The Children's Museum of Indianapolis
United States

Victoria Portway
Smithsonian National Air and Space Museum
United States

Mia Ridge
Museums Computer Group / Open University /
Open Objects Blog
United Kingdom

Ed Rodley
Peabody Essex Museum
United States

Adrianne Russell
Marianna Kistler Beach Museum of Art
United States

Suzanne Sarraf
National Gallery of Art
United States

Scott Sayre
Sandbox Studios
United States

Marsha Semmel
Noyce Leadership Institute /
Independent Consultant
United States

John Stack
Tate
United Kingdom

Len Steinbach
Steinbach and Associates
United States

Robert Trio
Hong Kong Maritime Museum
Hong Kong

Don Undeen
The Metropolitan Museum of Art
United States

John Weber
Institute of the Arts and Sciences, University of California, Santa Cruz
United States

Heather Marie Wells
Crystal Bridges Museum of American Art
United States

Bruce Wyman
Bruce Wyman & Associates
United States